A Sign

of

Faithfulness

A Sign of Faithfulness

Covenant & Baptism

H. Westerink

Translated by J. Mark Beach

INHERITANCE PUBLICATIONS
NEERLANDIA, ALBERTA, CANADA
PELLA, IOWA, U.S.A.

Canadian Cataloguing in Publication Data

Westerink, H.
  A sign of faithfulness

  Translation of: Een teken van trouw.
  ISBN 0-921100-00-0

  1. Baptism—Biblical teaching. I. Title.
  BV811.2.W47 1997   234'.161   C97-910885-3

Library of Congress Cataloging-in-Publication Data

Westerink, H.
  [Teken van trouw. English]
  A sign of faithfulness : covenant & baptism / H. Westerink.
            p.   cm.
  Includes index.
  ISBN 0-921100-00-0 (pb)
  1. Baptism—Biblical teaching. 2. Infant baptism—Biblical teaching. I. Title.
  BS2545.B36W4713   1997
  234'.161—dc21   97-35191
                                                                       CIP

Unless otherwise indicated, Scripture quotations are from *The Holy Bible, New King James Version*, copyright 1982, and are used with permission from Thomas Nelson Inc., Publishers.

Translated by J. Mark Beach

Originally published as *Een Teken van Trouw: over onze doop* (1987) by Uitgeverij De Vuurbaak, Barneveld, The Netherlands. Published with permission.

Cover Picture: *Niagara Falls* by Roelof A. Janssen

ISBN 0-921100-00-0

Published simultaneously in U.S.A. by Inheritance Publications
Box 366, Pella, Iowa 50219

Available in Australia from Inheritance Publications
Box 1122, Kelmscott, W.A. 6111 Tel. & Fax (09) 390 4940

Printed in Canada

Contents

TRANSLATOR'S PREFACE

H. Westerink's book on baptism is a jewel. One seldom comes across a book that simultaneously matches such simplicity to profundity, and vice versa. The author excels at clarifying the marvelous continuity (and discontinuity) between the old and new covenant with respect to the question of baptism — infant baptism in particular. Westerink's book honors the unity of God's written revelation as the author explores the meaning and relationship between circumcision and baptism. Thus, the reader is offered an approach to Scripture at direct odds with the dispensational theology so prominent in North American fundamentalism today. Rather than slice the Bible into so many separate sections (the dispensational approach), Westerink rightly handles Scripture as a harmonious revelation, wherein God reveals His everlasting covenant with His people and fulfills that covenant in Jesus Christ. Westerink beautifully shows the implications and applications of this covenantal perspective for baptism.

As for the translation itself, a few remarks are in order. First, since this book was originally written for a Dutch audience, some of the illustrations do not strictly apply to a North American setting. In the translation, on a few occasions, a small degree of editing was necessary in order to adapt the book for American and Canadian readers. Second, the translation reflects Westerink's fondness for referring to God as 'Lord' and 'LORD' — the latter being indicative of God's covenant name, *Yahweh*. The translation reflects Westerink's usage of these words.

A third matter concerns Westerink's frequent italicizing of words and phrases in Scripture-quotations. To observe each instance of this is undoubtedly proper grammatical etiquette, but would prove quite tedious for readers; thus it has not been done.

The translation of this book has a history. An initial draft was made by the Reverend Leo De Vos and appeared in successive issues of *The Trumpet,* beginning in January 1992. I have thoroughly re-worked the translation of Rev. De Vos and wish to thank him for his ground-breaking labors. I also wish to thank a few people who read all or part of the manuscript and offered helpful suggestions on matters of English style — namely, Mrs. Glenda Mathes, church secretary at the congregation I served in Pella, Iowa, Mrs. Val Van Kooten, instructor of English at Central College (Pella, Iowa), and Mr. John Barach, a graduate of Mid-America Reformed Seminary. I also wish to thank Dr. Nelson Kloosterman of Mid-America Reformed Seminary for his help in matters of translation and style. Responsibility for the translation remains mine, however.

It is my prayer that both pastors and people of the pew will be greatly blessed by this Scripture-saturated study on covenant and baptism, and that this book will be read with the Bible open (which is the author's intention). Our God is a covenant God, ever faithful. Recipients of His sign of promise are also recipients of His pledge of faithfulness. May believers find their assurance in the Lord.

J. Mark Beach
Mid-America Reformed Seminary
Dyer, Indiana, U.S.A.

AUTHOR'S PREFACE

This book is about our baptism and the assurance the LORD offers us in it, even if we were baptized as infants. It is essential that we understand our baptism well, especially since many oppose the necessity of infant baptism. Believers come to waver under such opposition, wondering whether they may find comfort in their baptism. Consequently, they start to look for assurance in their own hearts and lives, in their own feelings and experiences. But certainty will not be found there. It will be found only in constant instruction from God's Word, for that Word speaks clearly about the LORD's one covenant throughout human history.

Chapter One
SIGNS FROM GOD

Favor from the LORD

When you are young and in love, a richer, wider, and fuller world opens up before you, for you discover a heart that throbs just for you. There is another person who seeks and finds happiness in you. You begin to understand the meaning of the biblical proverb, "He who finds a wife finds a good thing, and obtains favor from the LORD" (Prov. 18:22). Yes, how true — "favor from the LORD."

Wedding Rings

So you get engaged and plan your wedding. You go to the jeweler and pick out your rings. During the wedding ceremony, you exchange vows, each saying, "I do." But are your words reliable? Aren't they unstable, floating in space? Don't your vows need to be tied down? So what do you do? You exchange rings. The rings serve as enduring signs. They're even made of enduring metal — gold! As you recite your vows, you place the rings on each other's fingers. In other words, you add to your invisible, floating words a visible, enduring sign. Your "I dos" and "rings" affirm the same thing: You are wed in the LORD. Your vows and rings pledge *faithfulness* to each other as in an oath — so help us God Almighty.

Such is the language of that sign — the sign of wedding rings.

*　　*　　*

People give signs to each other — such as wedding rings. But in the words of the medieval poem, *Beatrijs*, dating back at least six centuries: *There is so little fidelity in the world.*[1] Faithfulness is

---

[1] *Die werelt hout soe cleine trouwe. Beatrijs* is an anonymous lyric poem, written in an East Flemish dialect. It is regarded as the most outstanding of the medieval European Mary legends. The narrative is "the simple courtly tale of a nun who flees from the convent to marry a man she

precarious. We see that with our own eyes — divorce in the world and even in the church. So little fidelity. What good, then, is a sign? What good are marriage rings and marriage vows? Are they still of value?

I Am

Our words and signs have no more value than our fidelity to them. We know we cannot always count on others to keep their word. But when God speaks and offers a sign to accompany His Word, it is different. He is eternally faithful. Even His name declares it: *Yahweh* — I Am. I Am Who I Am (Ex. 3:14). God is not one thing today and something else tomorrow. He is always the same and keeps His promises. As the Psalmist wrote, ". . . Your faithfulness reaches to the clouds" (Ps. 36:5); also, ". . . the truth [faithfulness] of the Lord endures forever" (Ps. 117:2). So, too, when the believers at Corinth doubted the integrity of the apostle's words, he appealed to God's fidelity, "But as God is faithful, our word to you was not Yes and No" (2 Cor. 1:18).

Therefore, when God makes a promise to us, a sign isn't really necessary since He stands behind His Word for eternity. Indeed every word out of His mouth is like an oath, "for the Word of the Lord is right" (Ps. 33:4).

Signs for Others

As sinful people, however, we often consider God's Word inadequate. Thus, in His mercy, God offers signs to go along with His Word. We see many examples of this in Scripture. Noah received God's Word that the world would never again be destroyed by a flood, accompanied by the sign of the rainbow (Gen. 9:12-17). We have received that promise, too.

---

has loved from childhood. After fathering two children, he deserts her; she is forced into a life of sin, but remorse eventually drives her back to the convent where she discovers that she was not missed because the Virgin Mary had taken her place." — *Encyclopædia Britannica,* Micropædia, Volume 2 (Chicago: The University of Chicago, 1985), p. 17. —Trans.

God twice offered Gideon a sign: The woolen fleece soaked with dew, while the surrounding field was dry, and then the opposite — the fleece dry while the field was wet. This sign confirmed God's Word to Gideon that the Midianites would be delivered into his hands (Judg. 6:36-40).

King Hezekiah recovered from his terminal illness as the LORD had promised. But how did the king know this would happen? Along with the Word of God, he received a sign, namely, the shadow on the sundial went backwards ten degrees (2 Kings 20:8-11).

The shepherds in the fields of Ephrathah heard God's Word, too: "For there is born to you this day in the city of David a Savior, who is Christ the Lord." Then came a sign, "You will find a Babe wrapped in swaddling cloths, lying in a manger" (Luke 2:11-12).

In His public ministry Jesus performed many signs, the first of which took place at the wedding in Cana when He changed the water into wine. That was His first miraculous sign! "Jesus . . . manifested His glory; and His disciples believed in Him" (John 2:11). As the Lamb of God who takes away the sins of the world, Jesus manifested His glory through both words and miraculous signs! All His miracles functioned that way. They testified to Him. They *sign*ified who He was. They weren't tricks or feats of magic. They went with His gospel Word, confirming that Word in order to bring assurance of faith.

Thus when John comes to the end of his Gospel, he reaches back to the beginning and says, "And truly Jesus did many other signs in the presence of His disciples, which are not written in this book; but these are written that you may believe that Jesus is the Christ, the Son of God . . ." that is, so that you will see His glory "and that believing you may have life in His name" (John 20:30-31a).

Jesus' miracle at Cana is the first sign, with the result that the disciples put their faith in Him. So Jesus performed many miracles — many signs — so that we too will put our faith in Him and find life in His name. God's "signs" confirm His words. They are necessary not because God is unfaithful, but because the foolish are slow of heart to believe (Luke 24:25).

A Sign for Us

In the Belgic Confession we read that our gracious God, mindful of our insensitivity and infirmity, has ordained sacraments [signs] to seal His promises to us (*Belgic Confession*, Art. 33). He adds these signs to the Word of the gospel in order to make His promises clearer to us. Thus by a seal, a guarantee, He makes that word of promise more secure for us. Such is the sign of baptism.

This book is about the sign of baptism. Baptism remains a sign for us throughout our lives:

a sign when we are young and life is full of turmoil,
a sign when we struggle with sin and can't uproot it from our hearts,
a sign when despair overwhelms us because we commit the same
	sin over and over again,
a sign when we think there is forgiveness for everyone except
	ourselves,
a sign when our faith is attacked by a hostile world that lives and
	swears only by what can be seen or proven,
a sign in our every need — even when we are afraid and stand
	before a wall of sorrow, sickness, or death, when life is turned
	inside out,
a sign also in days of joy when life blossoms,
a sign for you and for me. For us!

Baptism is the sign and seal by which God takes pity on us. In it He strengthens our faith as often as necessary. And when is it not necessary? This sign gives us comfort and support so that we can find joy and happiness in Him.

But! — such comfort and support do not just drop into a person's lap. The LORD gives believers no license for laziness. Since He has given us His Word and sacraments, He requires (as is His right) that we listen to Him with faith and patience. He requires that we take the trouble to enter into His thoughts as He has revealed them to us in Scripture, for His thoughts are infinitely higher than our thoughts. Indeed, His thinking bears and supports our own (see Isa. 55:8).

Truly there is never a time when we don't need the strengthening of our faith — neither in our youth, nor in our middle years or old age, and certainly not in our dying hour when everything falls away and the only thing that remains is our last defense: The Word of God and the signs of God!

Chapter Two

SIGNS FOR ABRAHAM

Abraham is the father of all believers, which means he is our father (Rom. 4:11-12, 16-17). But his paternity did not come easily. He was a weak and sinful man. He declares his weakness by calling himself dust and ashes (Gen. 18:27); and his sinfulness is evident in that he had to be circumcised as one unclean (Gen. 17:10).

Great Promises

The LORD had promised Abraham great things: "I will make of thee a great nation" (Gen. 12:2, KJV). "To your descendants I will give this land [of Canaan]" (Gen. 12:7). "And in you all the families of the earth shall be blessed" (Gen. 12:3).

Abraham was seventy-five years old when God gave him those promises. Sarah, his wife, was sixty-five (Gen. 12:4; 17:7). Although she was childless, from now on she could look for a son in fulfillment of God's promise (Gen. 11:30).

But nothing happened. Nothing transpired which would indicate God's promise was being fulfilled. Years passed and nothing happened at all! How could Abraham and Sarah cling to God's promise? How could they believe His promise about a great nation? They were so old. What hope could they entertain (Rom. 4:18)? So Abraham said to God, "You have given me no offspring; indeed one born in my house — [a slave] — is my heir!" (Gen. 15:3).

Moreover, how could they cling to that other promise about the land? They had lived in tents for so long as strangers in that strange land. Abraham cried out, "Lord GOD, how shall I know that I will inherit it?" (Gen. 15:8). Abraham's words sound like a complaint. And since the promise about offspring and land had not been fulfilled, Abraham remained completely silent about the promise to become a blessing to all the families of the earth.

Stars and Animal Pieces

In the midst of these doubts the LORD helps Abraham. We read in Genesis 15 what God did. "Then He brought him outside and said, 'Look now toward heaven, and count the stars if you are able to number them.' And He said to him, 'So shall your descendants be' " (Gen. 15:5). So the LORD confirmed His promise. And Abraham "believed in the LORD, and He accounted it to him for righteousness" (Gen. 15:6). Thus, in the long years ahead, as often as Abraham looked up to the night sky, how he must have been encouraged in his faith. His seed would be like the stars!

*   *   *

But God wasn't finished. He did more. Next came the sign of the animal pieces. "So He said to him, 'Bring Me a three-year-old heifer, a three-year-old female goat, a three-year-old ram, a turtledove, and a young pigeon' " (Gen. 15:9). Abraham certainly could anticipate what was going to happen next. The LORD was going to cut a covenant with him. Abraham brought the animals and "cut them in two, down the middle, and placed each piece opposite the other" (Gen. 15:10). Such was the practice when two people made a covenant. The divided parts of the animals formed a bloody path. The parties of the covenant then walked together between the chopped up pieces of the animals. This meant that if one of them failed to keep covenant, may he be chopped into pieces like these animals. May the covenant breaker be cut in half!

Would the same hold true for the covenant between the LORD and Abraham? Would the LORD walk with Abraham between the divided animal parts? No! Only One would walk this bloody path. Thus we read, "And it came to pass when the sun went down and it was dark, that behold, there appeared a smoking oven and a burning torch that passed between those pieces" (Gen. 15:17). The smoking oven and burning torch symbolize the LORD. He walked the bloody path alone. Abraham cannot make a contribution. The certainty of this covenant could not depend on Abraham. It depended on the LORD and on Him alone. *There is so little fidelity in the world . . .* Yet, with the LORD . . . .

Yes, the LORD Himself passed between the pieces! God is saying, "If I fail to keep this covenant, may this happen to Me!" It's incomprehensible. How good God is! He made Himself the guarantee that Abraham would possess the land of Canaan. That was a guarantee Abraham could cling to with all his might. He could cling to God's word of promise and to the sign that went with it.

A New Sign for Abraham and his Descendants

As the years went by though, still nothing happened. In fact, fourteen years passed since the events of Genesis 15 (Gen. 16:6; 17:1). That's fourteen years of looking at the stars. Fourteen years of waiting, against all hope, for a faint glimmer of fulfillment (Rom. 4:18). Abraham turned ninety-nine. Sarah counted her eighty-ninth birthday (Gen. 17:24). Still no child. Still no land.

*   *   *

Again the LORD appeared to Abraham. The LORD said, "I am Almighty God" (Gen. 17:1). What a powerful name — *El-Shaddai!* As Almighty God, He came to *renew, enrich*, and *confirm* His covenant with Abraham. God *renewed* the promises: the descendants, the land, the blessing to the nations. He also *enriched* His covenant, calling it "an everlasting covenant, to be God to you and your descendants after you" (Gen. 17:7). Could it get any richer than that? What more could God give? And God *confirmed* His covenant. He certified and solidified it by means of a new sign — a sign which consisted of something more than counting stars or looking at animal pieces. This sign was not only for Abraham, but also for his descendants.

God's covenant promises were comprehended, or contained, entirely in this sign, for He said, "This is My covenant, which you shall keep, between Me and you and your descendants after you: Every male among you shall be circumcised . . . . So shall My covenant be in your flesh an everlasting covenant" (Gen. 17:10, 13b, RSV).

A Sign for All the Families of the Earth

But didn't circumcision then make the covenant too confined, too narrow, too nationalistic? Didn't that shrink the covenant to the tiny circle of Abraham and his people — a puny nation (Isa. 41:14)? Not really!

God's covenant extends beyond Abraham and his offspring. It extends to the ends of the earth. From the first time the LORD called Abraham, He promised him that all the families of the earth would be blessed through him (Gen. 12:3; 18:8; 22:18; 26:4; Acts 3:25; Gal. 3:8). And now, almost twenty-five years later, the LORD said it again, "I have made you a father of many nations" (Gen. 17:5).

We remember the mother promise God announced against the serpent in Genesis 3:15, "And I will put enmity between you and the woman, and between your seed and her Seed; He shall bruise your head, and you shall bruise His heel." The woman's Seed is Christ. And as those who live after the day of Christ, we also remember the great day of Pentecost when salvation was heard in the foreign languages of so many nations (Acts 2). Indeed, Abraham saw the day of Christ from afar, and was glad. He rejoiced in the divine salvation in Christ for "all the nations of the earth" (John 8:56; Heb. 11:13).

*   *   *

This is all contained in the sign of circumcision: the promise of a great nation, the promise of a great land. After all, what is a nation without land? The promise "I will be a God to you and to your descendants after you" is also contained in that sign, as is the promise that all the nations of the earth will be blessed — it's all there, for the day of Christ (Christ the Savior of the world, Immanuel, God with us) was guaranteed in this sign (Isa. 7:14; Matt. 1:23). This covenant contained everything — the full gospel. Even as it says in Scripture, "God . . . preached the gospel to Abraham beforehand, saying, 'In you all the nations shall be blessed' " (Gal. 3:8).

A Bloody Sign

New Testament believers do not undergo circumcision. Baptism has come in its place. When someone is baptized, whether as an infant or an adult, the ceremony is beautiful. Baptism is a beautiful sign. Maybe that leads us to think circumcision was beautiful, too. If it does, we are mistaken. Was it beautiful to be circumcised? Was it beautiful for a grown man or even a baby boy eight days old?

In Genesis 34, we read the shameful account of how the men of Shechem were circumcised under false pretenses. Do you remember what happened because they were circumcised? By the third day they were in so much pain that they were unable to defend themselves against the brutal attack of Simeon and Levi. They were helpless, and were slaughtered!

A beautiful sign?

*   *   *

You recall how the Israelites crossed the Jordan and placed their feet into Canaan. God's people in God's land! But during their forty years of wandering through the wilderness, the Israelites had not practiced circumcision. Imagine — the people of promise about to occupy the land of promise without the sign of promise. This must not be!

So the LORD arranged circumcision for the entire male population. He safeguarded Israel from her enemies during this time. Fear gripped the hearts of the Canaanites. News of Israel's crossing the Jordan made their hearts melt with fright. They had no courage left (Josh. 5:1); hence, there was a period of safety — time for circumcision and time for recovery. Thus we read, "When the circumcising of all the nation was done, they remained in their places in the camp until they were healed" (Josh. 5:8).

Really now, a beautiful sign?

A beautiful sign for a baby? In Exodus we learn how Moses lived in the land of Midian for forty years. He married a Midianite woman, Zipporah, and she bore him two sons. He named the eldest,

Gershom, for Moses was aware he was a stranger in a strange land.[2] He named his second son, Eliezer, which means, "My God is help." But though Moses had given his second son a beautiful name, along with it he had not given the "beautiful" sign. Moses had not circumcised him; thus he failed to uphold the everlasting covenant of God (that is, the covenant of the God who was his help!).

Shall Moses now lead God's people out of the house of bondage into the promised land? Never! In fact, we read that on his way back to Egypt the LORD was about to kill him, apparently because of his neglect of the covenant sign of circumcision.

Zipporah acted with haste and without urging. She "took a sharp stone and cut off the foreskin of her son and cast it at Moses' feet, and said, 'Surely you are a husband of blood to me!' . . . She said, 'You are a husband of blood!' because of the circumcision" (Ex. 4:24-26).

Is that a beautiful sign?

*　　*　　*

Have you ever visualized circumcision? Imagine an infant eight days old. The actual circumcision is about to be performed. The parents stand beside their baby. The sharp knife performs its task, cutting away the tender foreskin. There's blood! The baby screams! Mother can't bear to look. Father too has a difficult time — that's his little son. Days of throbbing discomfort await that child.

A beautiful sign? No! A bloody sign!

An Obsolete Sign

Under the Levitical laws of Moses, Israel became familiar with more bloody signs. For two thousand years a stream of blood flowed in sin offerings and guilt offerings, in the sacrifices of bulls and goats, rams and doves, and even in the blood of circumcised baby boys. God thus etched into the souls of His people this truth: *without satisfaction there can be no atonement for sin.*

---

[2] Gershom, in Hebrew, can be construed as *a stranger there.* —TRANS.

That's why in Exodus 24, after he read the book of the covenant to the people and they pledged to obey it, Moses "took the blood, sprinkled it on the people, and said, 'This is the blood of the covenant which the LORD has made with you according to all these words' " (Ex. 24:7-8). As the author of the letter to the Hebrews explains, "And according to the law almost all things are purified with blood, and without shedding of blood there is no remission" (Heb. 9:20-22). "The blood of the covenant" is the same covenant established with Abraham. Under Moses, however, it entered a new period.

The Lord Jesus was aware of Moses' words from Exodus 24. Undoubtedly, He was as aware of them as the author of Hebrews who quotes them. The Lord Jesus was also aware of the sign of circumcision that scarred His own body. As a twelve-year-old boy, busy with His Father's business, He saw the bloody animals sacrificed in worship to the Father. Already at that tender age the Holy Spirit taught Him that "it is not possible that the blood of bulls and goats could take away sins" (Heb. 10:4). Another blood — a better blood — was needed, a more powerful blood, unlike the blood of sacrificial animals which was never enough though poured out again and again (Heb. 10:1-3).

Do we fully realize what it means, then, when at the Last Supper the Lord Jesus said about the cup they shared, "Drink from it, all of you. For this is My blood of the new covenant, which is shed for many for the remission of sins" (Matt. 26:27, 28) — saying that with the words of Moses in His spirit (for He knew the Scriptures)? Do we fully grasp what happened at this table? Do we grasp that the Lord Jesus, who had to be baptized with that terrible baptism which would oppress Him until it was completed (Luke 12:50), at that moment announced the end of two thousand years of the shedding of blood?

Do we grasp that with these words of our Lord the stream of blood, which flowed for so many generations unto the forgiveness of their sins, would stop? Do we see how the Lord Jesus validated the new covenant and abrogated the old (Heb. 10:9) — how the bloody sign of circumcision has thus served its purpose? Do we see how in fact Jesus declared circumcision obsolete, and so it soon had to disappear (Heb. 8:13)?

Sin offerings and guilt offerings are now unnecessary (Heb. 10:18), for the Lord Jesus has said, "Behold, I have come to do Your will, O God" (Heb. 10:7, 9; Ps. 40:7-8). The Lord Jesus stood by God's will, which included, "For by one offering He has perfected forever those who are being sanctified" (Heb. 10:14). Indeed, now His blood has been shed for the forgiveness of sins.

Do we see how the Lord Jesus' institution of the new covenant in His blood brought the old covenant of Abraham and Moses to a new era, an era that required a new, bloodless sign? Do we see why baptism had to replace circumcision? We will consider this further in Chapter Eight, but notice here how the curtain was already being opened toward the new dispensation, the dispensation of Christ. That became clearly evident when God tore the curtain of the temple in two, from top to bottom, after His Son had said, "It is finished!" (Matt. 27:51; John 19:30). This happened less than twenty-four hours after Christ had instituted the new covenant in His blood.

In only a few weeks this became clear for all Israel, for on the day of Pentecost, which brought an end to the temple ministry and the Levitical priesthood, the Holy Spirit was poured out on that small band of disciples whom the Sanhedrin identified with the accursed multitudes, ignorant of the law (Acts 2:2; John 7:49).

The bloody sign of circumcision foreshadowed the day of Christ (John 8:56) — the day Abraham looked for from afar! That day requires a new sign, a bloodless sign — the sign of baptism, a baptism unto the forgiveness of sins (Acts 22:16). It's a sign for us.

> *Though your sins are like scarlet,*
> *They shall be as white as snow;*
> *Though they are red like crimson,*
> *They shall be as wool* (Isa. 1:18).

Chapter Three

THE LANGUAGE OF THE SIGN

The covenant sign of circumcision is expressed in these words: "This is My covenant . . . . Every male child among you shall be circumcised" (Gen. 17:10). "Abraham was ninety-nine years old when he was circumcised in the flesh of his foreskin" (Gen. 17:24).

The Riddle of the Sign

Abraham certainly knew what circumcision was. Circumcision was performed on boys — usually upon reaching maturity — among various peoples. The procedure involved cutting away a portion of the foreskin.

But why was this done? The answer resides in the belief ancient peoples had — namely, that circumcision removed an obstacle to fertility in marriage. Abraham was familiar with the practice, even though he had not been circumcised himself. Apparently his generation did not believe this operation was desirable in order to bring forth new life — and rightly so. Even when his marriage to Sarah remained fruitless and he was growing old, Abraham did not circumcise himself as a "means" to improve fertility.

But when he was almost a hundred years old, God told Abraham that he had to be circumcised — he and his household. From then on, every infant male-child of eight days old had to be circumcised. For what reason?

Must we assume that Abraham obeyed this command of God mindlessly, like a robot? Certainly not. Scripture acquaints us with "the father of all believers" in a much different way. We come to know him as a person who carefully considered what God said and did. The Bible gives us examples of this.

When the LORD told Abraham what He was going to do to Sodom and Gomorrah, Abraham reflected on this and wondered: Shall God destroy the righteous with the wicked? Even though he confessed himself as dust and ashes, he brought his questions before the LORD (see Gen. 18:22-23).

When Abraham and Sarah grew older and their bodies were wasting away, Abraham did not thoughtlessly ignore this fact. He took careful account of their age (Gen. 17:17; Rom. 4:19). By faith Abraham, the stranger in the land of promise, directed his attention to the heavenly homeland which he sought, even as "he waited for the city which has foundations, whose builder and maker is God" (Heb. 11:10, 15-16).

And when God asked him to offer up his son, his beloved son, Isaac, he considered that God by His power could raise the boy from the dead (Heb. 11:18).

*   *   *

So, in the same way, Abraham would have considered the matter of circumcision: "Why this sign? Why circumcision?"

Could his dead body receive new life by this sign — not to mention Sarah's barren womb? He knew better. Abraham knew that if a son of their flesh and blood — their *own son* — was ever to be born from their sexual union, this would be possible only by God's direct intervention, that is, the intervention of the Almighty who calls "those things which do not exist as though they did" (Gen. 15:4; Rom. 4:17).

Isn't this how it would be with the promised land? Hadn't the LORD made that clear earlier when He passed through the pieces of the chopped up animals by Himself? (see pages 17-18).

And thus it would also have to be with the promised child, for if that promise was to be fulfilled, dying bodies had to be made alive. Abraham did not waver in unbelief, wondering whether the LORD would perform this by His power (Rom. 4:17, 20-21).

But then, like a riddle, the question rang out with more urgency: Why the sign of circumcision? And with even more urgency: Abraham had to reflect on what God *said* about this sign.

Did God say that He would make Abraham's marriage fruitful through the sign of circumcision? No! It was not for the sake of a marriage relationship but for the sake of a covenant relationship that God opened a way and a future in the sign of circumcision. "This is My covenant . . . every male child among you shall be circumcised" — which means, the promise I pledge to you in My covenant I make visible and tangible in a lasting sign. For the rest of your life, and for the many centuries ahead, I bind My promise to your flesh and to the flesh of your descendants. I do it in that sign your foreign neighbors think removes an obstacle to fertility.

A Mark of Sin

With those words God has set the thinking of Abraham and his people on a covenantal track.

Did, then, an obstacle stand in Abraham's way to prevent him from having a covenant relationship with God? Did an obstacle stand in the way for his descendants?

Yes! The obstacle of *sin* was (and would remain) in the way — the sin that banished Adam and Eve from Paradise, that banished them from the tree of life, that banished them from the God of life. Whereas the mark of circumcision reminded pagan peoples of an obstacle of flesh and blood, God taught Abraham and his descendants to remember an obstacle in the depth of their hearts, the place where sin dwells. Moses prophesied of that when he said, "Therefore circumcise the foreskin of your heart, and be stiff-necked no longer" (Deut. 10:16).

As we have already observed, the sign of circumcision was not very pretty. It was bitter and bloody (see pages 21-23). The sin that circumcision testified to, however, was infinitely more bitter than the pain and blood of circumcision itself. For such sin is *enmity* toward God. It is *death!* The sign taught Abraham and Sarah, and Israel too, that in themselves they lay in the midst of death; and this was true of them not only as adults, but from the moment of their conception. As David wrote, "Behold, I was brought forth in iniquity, and in sin my mother conceived me" (Ps. 51:5).

Herein also lies the answer to the question: Why exactly that sign administered to the foreskin? Why not an incision in some other part of the body? And why a sign only on the husband and not on the wife? Because, according to God's ordering of things, a conception takes place first and foremost by a husband's desire (see John 1:13). As people say, the beginning of a "new life" lies within male virility — though properly speaking "life" does not reside in us, for with God alone is the fountain of life; in His light alone we see light (Ps. 36:9).

Indeed, without the LORD what holds true for Abraham, Sarah, Israel, and ourselves is this: In the midst of life we are in death.

A Mark of Reconciliation

Circumcision teaches us that God removes death. God removes death not only when we reach maturity as adults but immediately after we are born, so that immediately after we are born we may be covenant children. As He said, "He who is eight days old among you shall be circumcised" (Gen. 17:12). Already as infants they shall be allowed to bear in their little bodies the seal of the righteousness of faith (Rom. 4:11)! — for what is impossible with people is possible with God (Matt. 19:26).

The obstacle of sin, which people can never remove, God Himself removes by making atonement for sin. This is what the sign of circumcision guaranteed. The sign opened up a broad perspective, for blood flowed in each circumcision — blood that pointed forward to another blood which is better and more powerful than the blood of sacrificial animals and of little boys. The blood of circumcision taught people to look to the day of Christ, for there can be no reconciliation with God without satisfaction for sin. Truly, the wrath of God against sin is so great that, rather than leave it unpunished, He has punished it in His beloved Son, Jesus Christ, by the bitter and shameful death on the cross.[3] Christ's death brings reconciliation

---

[3] See "Form For the Celebration of the Lord's Supper," *Book of Praise: Anglo-Genevan Psalter, Revised Edition* (Winnipeg: Premier Printing, 1984), p. 594.

with God for Abraham and his people, too. In the bitterness and blood of circumcision, God gave His sign and His trustworthy seal of this reconciliation.

A Mark of New Life

But it is evident that the language of the sign has not yet been exhausted, for when God removed the obstacle of sin, did He then forsake the work of His hands? On the contrary, He brought it to completion, for His mercy endures forever (Ps. 138:8). He brought forth new life and said, "Walk before Me, and be blameless" (Gen. 17:1). That's unquestionably a command!

But God is not demanding a contribution from us beforehand. No contribution from our side will bring into being an agreement with God. God's covenant is no contract. He is the Initiator, and He is that all the way through. In the words of Isaiah 41, "I, the LORD, am the first; and with the last I am He" (Isa. 41:4).

Therefore we must understand that His command contains a promise, too. Would God make demands and not make one able to fulfill His demand, be it only a small beginning in this life? Would He remove death and not bring His own children to new life by His Spirit?

Abraham and his people then, by faith, did not stop at the outward sign. Moses spoke by faith when he impressed the same demand upon the people, "You shall love the LORD your God with all your heart, with all your soul, and with all your strength" (Deut. 6:5). And if they failed, if they forsook God's law and did not obey His voice or walk according to it, but walked according to the hardness of their heart, then how sourly would ring out the LORD's complaint, "Egypt, Judah, Edom, the people of Ammon, Moab . . . all these nations are uncircumcised, and [or, but] all the house of Israel are uncircumcised in the heart" (Jer. 9:26).

Many centuries later, we hear of the same reproach when Stephen stood before his judges who had rejected Christ. Being full of the Holy Spirit, Stephen reminded them of the covenant of circumcision (Acts 7:8). And he concluded his speech with those cutting words,

"You stiffnecked and uncircumcised in heart and ears! You always resist the Holy Spirit" (Acts 7:51; see Jer. 6:10). Indeed, they resisted the Spirit who gives life (John 6:63).

Paul too had the entire faith perspective of the Old Testament behind him when he wrote, "Circumcision is that of the heart, in the Spirit, and not in the letter . . ." (Rom. 2:29).

By faith Abraham and his people learned to understand the language of the sign of circumcision: a mark of *sin*, a mark of *reconciliation*, a mark of *new life*.

A Mark of God's People

Thus, through circumcision, God is the God of Abraham and his descendants; Israel is God's people. "The uncircumcised male child," however, "who is not circumcised in the flesh of his foreskin, that person shall be cut off from his people; he has broken My covenant" (Gen. 17:14).

What do we learn from that? We learn that the language of the sign can be summarized in a single word: *incorporation* That language speaks of incorporation into the holy people of God. It speaks of incorporation into His kingdom of priests (Ex. 19:6). And that incorporation pointed at once to the full gospel which, in the days of Abraham, was made visible and tangible with a lasting sign.

This benefit was for little ones who received the sign, though only eight days old. And it was for grown-ups who, as long as they lived, carried the mark of circumcision on their bodies as a sign of God's grace. This blessing was theirs if — if, with a believing heart, they accepted the blessing wherein the arm of the LORD was revealed to them (Isa. 53:1).

The Seal

But who has such great faith? Who can receive this great salvation? Who, of himself, has a firm grip on it? Who can appropriate God's promise to himself? Indeed, who dares? Who can rouse himself to it?

Absolutely nobody!

Therefore, because our gracious God was mindful of the insensitivity and infirmity of Abraham and his descendants, and the weakness of their faith, He instituted the sacrament of circumcision for them (see *Belgic Confession*, Art. 33). He did this in order to *seal* His promise to Abraham and his people. For, on the one hand, circumcision is a *sign*. Like a drawing in a sketchbook, this sign shows what God promises in His Word and what God will do in His people by His almighty power. Besides this, circumcision is also a *seal* — that is, a confirmation, an assurance, a guarantee. As the apostle said, "[Abraham] received the sign of circumcision, a seal of the righteousness of the faith which he had while still uncircumcised . . ." (Rom. 4:11).

If Abraham ever wavered in faith, if one of his descendants doubted whether he was truly righteous before God, if he wondered whether he truly belonged to the people of God, then this seal assured him of the righteousness of faith.

Righteousness means that God does not impute guilt. It means that death is removed, as if Abraham had never sinned nor been a sinner; as if he himself had accomplished all the obedience which Christ would accomplish for him (see *Heidelberg Catechism*, Q/A 60). Circumcision guaranteed this.

Thus Abraham and his descendants, possessing this seal wherein it was impossible that God should lie, had a powerful incentive to take hold of the hope that lay before them (see Heb. 6:18). And the child of Israel who reached out unto God's promise with a believing heart (though he sometimes had to cry out, "Help my unbelief"), that man could repeatedly look at the seal that was cut into his own flesh; for as surely as he bore that seal in his own flesh, so sure and certain was the word of promise from the God of Abraham, Isaac, and Jacob.

Boasting in the Lord

Thus, although circumcision brought *humility,* since every child of Israel was subject to death, it did not bring *despair.* It did not preach anyone into a pit, for circumcision clearly proclaimed that the God of the covenant removes death.

Circumcision made one *confident* to expect great things from the LORD. "Create in me a clean heart, O God, and renew a steadfast spirit within me" (Ps. 51:10), for all things are possible with God who is Almighty (Matt. 19:26).

Circumcision, however, did not make one *arrogant* — such as, once sealed always sealed! There was no such talk, for when God demands all your heart, soul, and strength, you are always guilty anew. Moreover, every year the great Day of Atonement was observed, and on that day Israel humbled herself with fasting and prayer (Lev. 16).

Besides confidence, God's sign of circumcision made one *joyful*, for it contained this promise, "And the LORD your God will circumcise your heart and the heart of your descendants, to love the LORD your God with all your heart and with all your soul, that you may live" (Deut. 30:6). Truly as a seal of the righteousness of faith, circumcision was the deepest cause of David's joyful jubilation:

> *Blessed is he whose transgression is forgiven,*
> *Whose sin is covered.*
> *Blessed is the man*
> *To whom the LORD does not impute iniquity* (Ps. 32:1-2).

For Israel's Redeemer also lived under the old covenant (Job 19:25), and His sign and seal had been cut into the flesh of God's people. Abraham had looked for His day from afar — the day of Christ (John 8:56). And Abraham saw it! Yes, he really saw that day, for he could see God's compassion directed toward his own life and the lives of his descendants (Heb. 11:16). God was not ashamed to be called his God and the God of his children.

Who else could this be than Immanuel, God with us, God with His people (Matt. 1:23; Isa. 7:14)? Who else could it be in light of the fact that Christ willed to become, for Abraham and his descendants, wisdom from God — that is, their righteousness, sanctification, and redemption (1 Cor. 1:30)?

Truly everything, the full gospel, was comprehended in God's covenant word and covenant sign (Gal. 3:8). Thus the words that were true in the old dispensation, would be true also in the new dispensation: "He who glories, let him glory in the LORD" (1 Cor. 1:31; Jer. 9:24).

Chapter Four
GOD'S OWN PEOPLE

Under the old covenant, anyone who was circumcised belonged to the people of God. Is it necessary to consider this further? Would the same hold true for the sign of the new covenant, for baptism? So why, you ask, do we pay so much attention to a covenant sign now over four thousand years old?

The Same Yesterday and Today

Why? Because God is the same yesterday, today, and forever (Heb. 13:8), because He does not faithlessly abandon the work of His hands. That's why! Certainly we can see progression in God's words and signs; we see development and fulfillment. But we do not see disjunction or rupture, let alone contradiction or opposition.

God is the same God under the new covenant as He was under the old covenant. As He was a compassionate God then, He is a compassionate God now. His covenant is one and unbroken, for He is one, "I AM WHO I AM" (Ex. 3:14).

Therefore, if you wish to be comforted by your baptism today, as well as strengthened in faith by it, you must go back to the beginning. And although that will require both patience and exertion from you, it's not impossible. After all, feasting on the bread of life is not the same as a quick bite at a fast-food outlet. It's to obediently pull up your chair to the feast which is the Word — the feast which God prepared from of old. In this way you become wise (Ps. 19:7). In other words, you must learn what God has to say from the whole Bible.

Creational Bonds

So what does the Bible teach us? It teaches that God created the heavens and the earth and that He created man as His vice-regent on the earth. He created the man and then created the woman as a helper suitable for him. She was like the left hand matching the right hand (Gen. 2:18). Male and female God created them — of equal worth, each complementing the other (Matt. 19:4). What significance does this have for our topic — that is, for understanding covenant, circumcision, and baptism?

Among other things, it shows that from the very beginning the man and woman had the mandate to be fruitful and multiply, and fill the earth. They were called to have children, form a family, and in turn their children would form families! The LORD wanted family bonds. He wanted generations of children, parents, and grandparents. He wanted races and nations. From one human pair He wanted a united human race in His service (Acts 17:26). All of this lay embedded in the creation as part of His plan. The human race would arise in this way.

Adam could not fulfill this mandate by himself, nor could the woman do it alone. Only together could they fulfill the mandate (1 Tim. 2:14).

We don't know how life would have developed if the fall into sin had not occurred, for that great tragedy did occur; the fall into sin did happen. And at that very moment the woman ceased to be a suitable helper for Adam. She withdrew herself from the man and walked headlong into evil, "She took of its fruit and ate. She also gave to her husband with her, and he ate" (Gen. 3:6). Then Adam withdrew himself from the wife he once had received with such joy, and pointed the accusing finger, "The woman whom You gave to be with me, she gave me of the tree, and I ate" (Gen. 3:12).

Thus, nothing less than the unity between them was broken. Decay entered this marriage as decay enters a corpse. Decay entered the whole world. We see this decay at work when Cain murdered Abel (Gen. 4:1-9). We see it when Lamech bragged about revenge in his song: "for I have killed a man for wounding me, even a young man for hurting me" (Gen. 4:23). The human race started falling apart. Human history is full of such tragedy right up to the present day. The black veil of death covers life — this is decay!

Disposable Junk?

What then? What did God do? Did He forsake the work of His hands (Ps. 138:8)? Did He forsake His creation? Did He forsake Adam and His wife? Did He forsake His divine mandate to be fruitful and multiply? Did He let go of family bonds, family relations, and generations — that is, the family lines which were part of His plan from the beginning?

No! Rather than forsake His creation, God prepared to cast off the veil that covered all peoples, as well as the sheet that was spread over all nations. He would destroy forever the last enemy — death (Isa. 25:7). He would wipe away the tears, once and for all (Isa. 25:8; Rev. 21:4). In the midst of death, God provided new life. The first paradise was lost. A paradise restored shall come. Ever since the fall God has been busy pursuing this goal.

*   *   *

How is God doing this, you wonder? Did He do it by following a skinny dotted line, made up of a few saved souls here and an individual saved soul there, ignoring family bonds and generational lines? No! This was not what He did. God did not forsake the work of His hands. He wasn't at a loss about what to do with the bonds He established in the created order: marriage, family, and generations. How could God, the Almighty, be at a loss about what to do? God reestablished peace by putting enmity between the serpent and the woman, between the serpent's seed and the woman's Seed (Gen. 3:15). Hence there are two seeds — the seed of the serpent and the Seed of the woman. But don't fail to notice — there is *seed!*

What does this mean? It means God maintains the original mandate He gave, to be fruitful and multiply, and fill the earth. It means He restores the marriage bonds and the marital fellowship between man and woman. We see this immediately. Adam leads the way by giving the woman a new name: *Eve.* For God opens new horizons. Eve means *life.* This is the woman's new name. She shall be the mother of all the living (Gen. 3:20).

Thus, the family comes into the picture again. Family relationships, with a father and a mother, appear once more on the horizon. We see generational lines silhouetted against the sky. Races and nations do not disappear from God's family circle like so much disposable junk. On the contrary, He enlists them in His work of salvation — the work of salvation that shall span the centuries.

No, God's plan has not changed because of the fall. God never has to change His plans in light of new facts or developments. God never has to "make do" with patching something together from pieces of junk. He is Almighty! He wanted family bonds from the very beginning. He knew from eternity what He was doing and why He was doing it. From eternity He could see the Holy Spirit governing the lives of children through the instrumentality of parents.[4]

God never has to make do with what just happens "by chance" to be there. For God not only creates but, according to His counsel, He creates what He wills *to use*. The Lord arranges one thing to fit with another. Thus, the covenant relationship fits with family bonds and vice versa.

It's true that the fall radically altered things. But the Lord did not lose control. He continued to deal with Adam and Eve and their family line. Later, Cain also belonged to that family tree. In the same way, God rescued Noah's family through the flood. That included Shem. And then for many centuries, yes, God confines the stream of life to the narrow banks of Abraham and his family line. He did not want to deal with any other nation (Ps. 147:20). And the nations had only themselves to blame for that. Remember the tower of Babel? And yet, already when He called Abraham away from his family and homeland, God had in mind "all the families of the earth" (Gen. 12:3).

And if we ask in what way God would do this, the answer is quite clear, "I will make you a great nation" (Gen. 12:2) — meaning that the LORD enlisted Abraham and Sarah. He again used man and woman, male and female, a household, a family, and descendants.

---

[4] See "Form For the Baptism of Infants," *Book of Praise: Anglo-Genevan Psalter*, p. 584.

He used Isaac and Rebekah, Jacob and his two wives, Leah and Rachel. He used the servant girl, Bilhah, and the handmaid, Zilpah. God uses families and their descendants. And God's covenant certainly included those who were stiff-necked and uncircumcised in heart and ears. We see them from Esau to Caiaphas and beyond (Acts 7:51). But along this path God forms a people — His people! And along this path, too, His salvation comes to the nations; indeed, to all the families of the earth.

God's Own People

We should not belittle this way of salvation which travels along the path of family bonds, or speak disparagingly of it by saying, "Sure that was mostly (if not entirely) an external affair, merely a matter of flesh and blood." Neither may we dismiss the sign of circumcision as if it were only a sign of nationality. Unfortunately, there are people, Christian people, who do that.

If we think that way, we contradict the LORD Himself. He told Abraham that the sign of circumcision was the identification mark of His people (Gen 17:14). It was not just a formal thing, an outward mark. No, it was wholly and completely, one hundred percent, body and soul, the identification mark of God's people. It was the identification mark of His covenant (Gen. 17:14).

God was not and is not double-tongued. He doesn't keep two different nations within His covenant simultaneously. He doesn't have one nation outwardly and then another nation inwardly — as if a tiny, spiritual nation constituted His genuine possession within the borders of an outward nation.

When the Lord spoke to Moses at the burning bush, He said, "I have surely seen the oppression of My people who are in Egypt" (Ex. 3:7). God called them *My people!* And that was not merely in name. Indeed, you can't miss it, especially when God confronted Pharaoh, for Moses had to go to Pharaoh and tell him, "Thus says the LORD: 'Israel is My son, My firstborn. So I say to you, let My son go' " (Ex. 4:22-23). "My son!" "My firstborn!" "Let My son go!" And in the struggle between Moses and Pharaoh, between the LORD and Satan, we hear that language again and again. Again and again we hear, "Let My people go" (Ex. 5:1; 8:1, 20; 9:13; 10:3). *My people!* Yes! — for the situation will become more terrible for Israel.

Pharaoh refused to provide Israel the straw with which to make her regular quota of bricks, and so her taskmasters beat her mercilessly. The Israelites complained that Moses and Aaron had managed only to make their situation worse than ever. Thus when Moses brought their complaint to God, and said, "Lord, why have You brought trouble on this people" (Ex. 5:22), then the LORD replied, "Now you shall see what I will do to Pharaoh" (Ex. 6:1). They would see it with their own eyes!

The LORD reminded Moses of His covenant with Abraham, Isaac, and Jacob, and He reminded him of His great name: "I am the LORD [*Yahweh*]. I appeared to Abraham, to Isaac, and to Jacob, as God Almighty, but by My name LORD I was not known to them" (Ex. 6:2-3). The patriarchs did not know the LORD by what we properly call the covenant name of God. What God had kept hidden in that name, He revealed there and then to His people, namely, His unchanging faithfulness (see Mal. 3:6).

God sent Moses to the people to bring His words to them, "I will take you as My people, and I will be your God" (Ex. 6:7). The phrase "take you as My people" seems peculiar. Does Israel become God's people only now? Hadn't they become His people much earlier? Yes! They had become His people much earlier (see Ex. 3:7; also Gen. 17:4; 12:2). But because the enemy now advances, the LORD will make clear to every eye that Israel is His people. In fact, God makes it so clear that inhabitants as far away as Jericho and Gibeon will be talking about it forty years later: "For we have heard how the LORD dried up the water of the Red Sea for you when you came out of Egypt . . ." (Josh. 2:10; 9:9). He will now give Israel everything she needs from Him — deliverance from Egypt, freedom from the house of bondage, and redemption from the power of death and decay.

Consequently, the ten plagues followed. The situation was turned upside down, so to speak; for the firstborn son of God, Israel, was an eyewitness to the death of the firstborn of Egypt. Soon after that, Israel also saw the Egyptian army lying dead on the shores of the Red Sea.

In light of God's mighty deliverance of His people, was circumcision then just an outward ordinance? Was it just an outward mark of the flesh needed in order to belong to God's people? Was it merely a national insignia and not a spiritual reality? If that were the case, then how could Israel sing the Song of Moses on the shores of the Red Sea?

> *The LORD is my strength and song,*
> *And He has become my salvation* (Ex. 15:2).

Looking back many years later, Moses chose a very tender image to depict God's relationship with His people. He remembered God's love, His constant faithfulness and care for Israel, and he said, "you saw how the LORD your God carried you, as a man carries his son, in all the way that you went until you came to this place" (Deut. 1:31).

And many centuries later, when Israel was in exile with no apparent hope of returning to her homeland, the LORD Himself referred back to that image of Moses. For He said through Isaiah the prophet, "Listen to Me, O house of Jacob, and all the remnant of the house of Israel, who have been upheld by Me from birth, who have been *carried from the womb*" (Isa. 46:3).

The LORD did not break off His relationship with Israel — not even when she was living in exile and getting everything she deserved. No! — for Babylon had to carry her own god on her shoulders: "They bear it on the shoulder, they carry it and set it in its place, and it stands; from its place it shall not move. Though one cries out to it, yet it cannot answer nor save him out of his trouble" (Isa. 46:7). How very different things were between the LORD and His people, for the Lord promised, "Even to your old age, I am He [for *Yahweh* means *I Am*], and even to gray hairs I will carry you! I have made, and I will bear; even I will carry, and will deliver you" (Isa. 46:4).

And if a person asks how the LORD could be so good to Israel, the answer can be found in Moses' last instructions to Israel in the book of Deuteronomy. For there Moses told Israel that ". . . the LORD has taken you and brought you out of the iron furnace, out of Egypt, to be His people, an inheritance, as you are this day" (Deut. 4:20; 7:6). God's very own people! Is it possible to be closer to God? As we have already said many times before, this was the full gospel for the men, women, and children of Israel, for to them "belongs the adoption as sons and the glory and the covenants and the giving of the Law and the temple service and the promises" (Rom. 9:4).

As death has worked its way through all the descendants of Adam (Rom. 5:12), so God, according to the depths of His riches, wisdom, and holiness, opened a road of life among the people of Israel. And that is certainly something much more than a matter of blood and nationality.

Chapter Five

CHILDREN OF GOD'S PEOPLE

A nation includes children. The LORD knows that very well when He uses the phrase "My people." He does not quietly exclude them from His covenant promises but speaks of men, women, *and children*. Had He not used the image of a *people*, He would have acted deceitfully.

Thus the children in Israel were not left dangling. It wasn't the case that, whereas their parents belonged to the people of God, Israel's children were in the same class as the children of heathens. The children in Israel were not like a blank sheet of paper awaiting someone's handwriting either, being somewhere in between God's people and pagans, so that their parents had to wait to see which way they would tip the scales: toward the people of God or toward the pagans.

A Sacrament of Jesus Christ

No! Israel's children lived under grace. The LORD Himself did not allow a single doubt about that. At His command, every boy was circumcised eight days after birth. And this sign from God — which spoke of sin, atonement, conversion, and incorporation into the people of God — was not powerless, so that Israel was misled. God promised to carry that child even as a man carries his own child (see *Belgic Confession*, Art. 33; Deut. 1:31).

*   *   *

But that was not all, for according to the Levitical stipulations, shortly after the birth of a child — whether a girl or a boy — the child's mother had to bring two offerings for herself and her child: a young pigeon or a turtledove as a sin offering and a lamb as a burnt offering (Lev. 12:6, 8; see Luke 2:24).

41

Why a *sin offering?* Because atonement had to be made for mother and child, since from the moment of conception sin brings a separation between the LORD who is on one side, and the mother and child who are on the other.

Why a *burnt offering?* Because this offering had to be brought as a pleasing odor to the LORD and as a sign of devotion to Him. The newborn life was for the LORD (Lev. 1:13, 17).

Blood was shed in both the sin offering and the burnt offering. The language of both offerings was the same as circumcision: sin had to be atoned for through the shedding of blood. That was the foremost message! In addition to this — and closely connected to this — there was also the message that life, new life, is devoted to the LORD. Thus the blood that was shed in circumcision, and in "birth" offerings as well, pointed to the blood of "the Lamb of God, who takes away the sin of the world" (John 1:29).

For this reason, the church confesses that the burnt offering of the lamb was a "sacrament of Jesus Christ" — a sign and seal of Him (*Belgic Confession,* Art. 34). And so, as in circumcision, so also in the promise of God and in the symbolism of offerings (wherein it was impossible that God would mislead His people), parents and children had a firm anchor that God accepted them as His nation — a nation of fathers, mothers, and children (Heb. 6:18).

They are children under grace.

Inquisitive Children

God abundantly proved that grace to His people when He led them out of Egypt. He proved it to adults and children together (Ex. 12:37). Passover was the abiding sacrament of this gracious event. It was a sacrament of deliverance.

At the Lord's command, every father and mother in Israel had to tell their children of that deliverance, for God does not permit educational opportunities to be neglected. He sets up these opportunities so that the children may be nurtured and grow up into adulthood (Ps. 71:17). Thus "when your children say to you, 'What do you mean by this service?' you shall say, 'It is the sacrifice of the LORD's passover, for He passed over the houses of the people of Israel in Egypt, when He slew the Egyptians but spared our houses.' " (Ex. 12:26-27).

Notice it says *our houses*. Children lived in those houses and were graciously spared, too. And later, when the children heard about this deliverance from the lips of their parents, they certainly understood that they belonged to "our houses."

They are children under grace.

*   *   *

After Israel was delivered from the house of slavery, she could serve the LORD as a free nation. She was to celebrate her freedom on a feast day, specifically the Feast of Unleavened Bread. This feast followed right after the Passover feast. Passover lasted one evening. The Feast of Unleavened Bread, however, lasted for seven days. During that period Israel ate bread without leaven.

Leaven was old dough which was intentionally kept out of the batch of dough from the previous day. In the warm climate of the Middle East, such dough would begin to ferment quickly. Thus it would soon sour That dough was kneaded into a fresh batch of dough (as in the way we use yeast) so that the new dough would rise. Soon the fresh dough was leavened.

With the hasty exodus from Egypt, it would have taken too much time to let the bread ferment with leaven. Israel had to take their dough before it was leavened (Ex. 12:34, 39).

The LORD now used this incident to instruct His people — even for the future. In observance of the feast of unleavened bread this rule applied for centuries: "And no leavened bread shall be seen among you, nor shall leaven be seen among you in all your quarters" (Ex. 13:7).

Why? Again this was a *sign!* This was a sign that sin, that which is old and decaying, must be eradicated from the life of God's people. Scripture speaks of this in the New Testament: "Do you not know that a little leaven leavens the whole lump? Therefore purge out the old leaven, that you may be a new lump, since you truly are unleavened. For indeed Christ, our Passover, was sacrificed for us" (1 Cor. 5:6-7).

Passover and the Feast of Unleavened Bread were again the gospel of God, who atones for sin and quickens unto new life. The children participated in the celebration of that annual feast. They too ate the strange, unleavened bread. If they were still ignorant of its significance, well then, as God had commanded fathers: "And you shall tell your son in that day, saying, 'This is done because of what the LORD did for me when I came up from Egypt.' It shall be as a sign to you on your hand and as a memorial between your eyes, that the Lord's law may be in your mouth; for with a strong hand the LORD has brought you out of Egypt" (Ex. 13:8-9).

"The LORD has brought *you* out of Egypt" — "you" means the children! So the lips of fathers were to testify to their children.

They are children under grace.

*   *   *

And this command applied not only to these two feasts; it applied to all of God's statutes and commandments. "When your son asks you in time to come, saying, 'What is the meaning of the testimonies, the statutes, and the judgments which the LORD *our* God has commanded you?' then you shall say to your son: '*We* were slaves of Pharaoh in Egypt' " (Deut. 6:20-21a). "We" means "our people." Again, children, without their knowledge, belong to God's people — just as, without their knowledge, they belonged to the people of God when the LORD made a covenant with their father, Abraham; just as, without their knowledge, they share in Adam's condemnation.[5] As Deuteronomy 6 continues, "you shall say to your son, '. . . and the LORD brought *us* out of Egypt with a mighty hand . . . . Then it will be righteousness for *us*, if we are careful to observe all these commandments before the LORD *our* God, as He has commanded *us*' " (Deut. 6:21b, 25).

"It will be righteousness for us . . . ."

---

[5] See "Form For the Baptism of Infants," *Book of Praise: Anglo-Genevan Psalter*, p. 584.

How? Will this happen mechanically or automatically? Was one circumcised and therefore justified? Are they *children under grace* and thus saved forever?

Absolutely not!

It will be righteousness for us "if we are careful to observe all these commandments before the LORD our God." It will be righteousness for us as Abraham was reckoned righteous when he believed in the LORD, so that he could be the father of the circumcised; for Abraham is the father of those who walk in his footsteps of faith (Gen. 15:6; Rom. 4:12).

They are children under grace.

Talking Stones

It is striking how again and again the LORD thinks specifically about the *children* of His people. After He led His people with a strong hand through the Jordan, then twelve men, one from each tribe, were instructed to select a stone from the middle of the river and place it on their shoulders. At Gilgal these stones were piled upon one another as a sign. Notice that again — as a sign!

And "When your children ask their fathers in time to come, saying, 'What are these stones?' then you shall let your children know, saying, 'Israel crossed over this Jordan on dry land;' for the LORD *your* God dried up the waters of the Jordan before *you* until *you* had crossed over, as the LORD your God did to the Red Sea, which He dried up before us until we had crossed over" (Josh. 4:7, 21-23).

We see it now, don't we? We're paying close attention, right? The text says that the LORD *your* God dried up the waters before *you* until *you* crossed over. "You" means the covenant children! Without their knowledge, they crossed over the Jordan and the Red Sea on dry ground.

They are children under grace.

My Children

In Isaiah 38 we read how King Hezekiah was healed of a fatal illness and how his heart brimmed over with gratitude. Consequently, he spoke of the Lord's grace and faithfulness shown to him:

> *It is the living who gives thanks to Thee, as I do today;*
> *A father tells his sons about Thy faithfulness* (Isa. 38:19, NASB).

Hezekiah's thinking was also piously shaped *along generational lines.* For Israel's children had to live under the grace which God had once shown to His people — and yet showed to them every day.

*   *   *

And who can doubt that after hearing with Ezekiel the burning indignation of the Lord concerning the spurning of His great love? Thus the Lord said, "Moreover you took your sons and your daughters, whom you bore to Me, and these you sacrificed to them [i.e., to your idols] to be devoured. Were your acts of harlotry a small matter, that you have slain *My children* and offered them up to them [to idols] by causing them to pass through the fire?" (Ezek. 16:20-21).

Notice: God called them "My children." They were His own children!

Children Under the Law

Asaph, the poet of Psalm 78, was familiar with the history of God's people. He summons the Lord's people (he too belonged among them!) to hear a lesson from history — a lesson which he proceeds to tell. Asaph understood that God's people did not consist of adults only. He knew of the Lord's care for *the children.* He knew of God's command that parents must tell their children about the Lord's mighty acts in history. Asaph experienced the blessing of that instruction in his own life (Ps. 78:1) — things "which we have heard and known, and our fathers have told us" (Ps. 78:3).

He gained his knowledge from this instruction. In the same way, he in turn passed on that knowledge:

> *We will not hide them from their children,*
> *Telling to the generation to come the praises of the* Lord,
> *And His strength and His wonderful works*
> *That He has done* (Ps. 78:4).

Then, continuing with the psalm, Asaph tells about the Lord who established a witness in Jacob:

> *He established a testimony in Jacob,*
> *And appointed a law in Israel,*
> *Which He commanded our fathers,*
> *That they should make them known to their children;*
> *That the generation to come might know them,*
> *The children who would be born,*
> *That they may arise and declare them to their children,*
> *That they may set their hope in God . . .* (Ps. 78:5-7a).

Asaph learned to think along generational lines also with respect to God's law. He learned this not from a stranger but from God Himself: "You shall teach them [God's commandments] to your children, speaking of them when you sit in your house, when you walk by the way, when you lie down, and when you rise up" (Deut. 11:19; see 6:7).

*   *   *

For this reason, the children also had to be present when the law was read once every seven years, according to the command of Moses. "Gather the people together, men and women and *little ones*, and the stranger who is within your gates, that they may hear and that they may learn to fear the Lord your God and carefully observe all the words of this law, and that their *children*, who have not known it, may hear and learn to fear the Lord your God" (Deut. 31:12-13a).

And later, when the people assembled in front of Mount Ebal and Mount Gerizim, and Joshua read all the words of the law — again according to the law of Moses — including the blessings and the curses, the "little ones" were among "all the assembly of Israel" (Josh. 8:35).

*   *   *

Do the "little ones" of God then have cause for complaint? Are they, already in their youth, like slaves groaning under the exacting commandments of an exacting taskmaster? Does sonship with God include a bright side (grace) as well as a dark side (law)?

Certainly not!

For when the LORD translates people from death to life, and gives reliable signs of that to parents and children, He does not then give them over to the license of their own hearts, nor does "new life" before the LORD become simply a matter of one's own (faulty) insight. Thus it is not the case that a person may rightly say, "I think that you should live this way," while someone else just as rightly says, "But I think another way is better."

What mother raises her children like that, without rules? What father allows his sons to run wild, with no clear instructions? What teacher fails to have a clear code of behavior for his students?

"Teacher" is the word that is translated "tutor" in the letter to the Galatians. Scripture teaches us there that the law was Israel's pedagogue — that is, tutor — to bring us to Christ (Gal. 3:24-25). In ancient times the pedagogue was the man who brought the children to school and who also instructed and admonished them. As their caring attendant, he also disciplined them. And discipline certainly is not a matter of harsh words and a strict hand in the church of the living God. It is a matter of leading and attracting, of exerting pressure, and even threatening and punishing when necessary — but always a pressing forward toward the Lord.

We must not separate God's law — that teacher — from God's grace, and certainly not set the law of God against the grace of God. "So then, the Law is holy, and the commandment is holy and righteous and good" (Rom. 7:12). How could it be otherwise? Is not the law-giver God Himself? Is not God holy and just and good? God is not partly a god of grace and partly a god of hard-nosed justice. He is gracious — altogether a God of grace. And He is just — altogether a God of justice. In Him one attribute is not in conflict with another, for ". . . God is light and in Him is no darkness at all" (1 John 1:5).

> *The law of the LORD is perfect,*
> *reviving the soul* (Ps. 19:7, RSV).

God's law is not a heavy burden, but a law of *love*. As the Lord Jesus said, "You shall love the LORD your God with all your heart, with all your soul, and with all your mind" and "You shall love your neighbor as yourself" (Matt. 22:37, 39). This shall be in your heart. This is what you shall instill in your children.

To be sure, when the LORD unfolded His law of love into Ten Commandments at Mount Sinai, this happened amid claps of thunder, flashes of lightening, the sound of a trumpet, and the mountain smoking (Ex. 20:18). The people trembled and stood at a distance. They said to Moses, "if we hear the voice of the LORD our God anymore, then we shall die . . . . You go near and hear all that the LORD our God may say, and tell us all that the LORD our God says to you, and we will hear and do it" (Deut. 5:25, 27). Indeed, so awesome was this sight that Moses himself said, "I am exceedingly afraid and trembling" (Heb. 12:21). Most certainly he was trembling!

But we may not play off the majesty of God, displayed in the giving of the law, against the grace of God. We may not minimize His grace in order to maximize the goodness and holiness of His law. The LORD does not want that to happen, for Moses had to go to the people and say, "Do not fear . . . ."

"Do not fear; for God has come to test you, and that His fear may be before you, so that you may not sin" (Ex. 20:20). Thus God instills fear, reverence, and awe.

God's pedagogue takes God's people by the hand. In the words of Isaiah, "Your ears shall hear a word behind you, saying, 'This is the way, walk in it,' whenever you turn to the right hand or whenever you turn to the left" (Isa. 30:21). The law was given as Israel's pedagogue so that she might not disturb her fellowship with God through sin, with the consequence that those who were called "His people" would become "no longer His people," and those who were called "His sons" would become "no longer His sons" (see Hos. 2:23; Rom. 9:25-26).

What else is this than the old law of the covenant with Abraham? Isn't this the law that stated, "Walk before Me, and be blameless" (Gen. 17:1)? Isn't this the law from the very beginning in Paradise: "but of the tree of the knowledge of good and evil you shall not eat" (Gen. 2:17)? By trusting in your Creator "you shall not eat" — that alone renders His command truly wise and fitting.

Such are blessed people! Such also are blessed children!

Chapter Six

OLD COVENANT - NEW COVENANT

Israel had been God's own people for two thousand years. The children in Israel were God's own sons and daughters, too. Would it be different in the new dispensation? Would it be different with the inauguration of a better covenant, resting on better promises, a new covenant when the LORD would put His law in their minds and write it on their hearts instead of on stone tablets, when He would renew His pledge of assurance, even using the words of the old covenant, "and I will be their God, and they shall be My people" (Heb. 8:6-11; see Jer. 31:31-34), when the least of them to the greatest would know Him? Would God's covenant be different in the new dispensation? With the inauguration of the new covenant, would the children henceforth be excluded? Is that how it is in the kingdom of God? Does the LORD change — actually change? Does He forget His grace which He always showed to Abraham and his descendants (Ps. 77:9)?

The Promise of Pentecost

We can raise these same questions in another way. On the day of Pentecost, did the Holy Spirit, with Peter as His mouthpiece, set aside the ordinances of the Creator, the ordinances God Himself expressly upheld even after the fall? Does He negate His statutes toward Adam and Eve? Toward Abraham (Gen. 3:15; 17:7; see also 5:2-3)? Is the way of salvation, along which God's people walked for twenty centuries, now broken up on the great day of Pentecost? Is the way of "you and your descendants" abolished? Absolutely not! For is it not appalling to think that the hand of the Almighty should change (see Ps. 77:10, NASB)?

51

On Pentecost, Peter preached the gospel of the divine Abrahamic promise *also* to the "men of Israel" (Acts 2:22; Gal. 3:8). He did not call them "men and brethren" for nothing, certainly not just to be polite (Acts 2:29). With this form of address, he reminded them that they, along with the apostles, were really sons of God (Deut. 32:6). He evoked for his hearers the entire relationship between God and His people as it had existed for centuries. And when, because of his words, they were cut to the heart and asked the apostles, "Men and brethren, what shall we do" (notice now the same form of address from their side), then Peter showed them the way to Christ (Acts 2:37). And in direct connection with that Peter said to them, "For the promise is to you and to your children . . ." (Acts 2:39).

Which promise? The promise of the Holy Spirit. Joel prophesied of it, and he didn't do so carelessly or without proper grounds. Rather, he did this with steadfast faith in the LORD, who had been zealous for His *land* and *people* (Joel 2:18). In other words, when Joel prophesied, he stood on the firm foundation of God's promises to Abraham.

The three thousand souls who were baptized and added to the church on the day of Pentecost belonged to the same people whom God had taught for centuries to think along generational lines. Not one of them could — or should — have understood their baptism and assimilation into the church as anything other than as being part of the same line of God's eternal covenant with Abraham. It was not anything different — not then, not later, and not even today. For they all knew God who called Himself, "Yahweh — I AM WHO I AM," who is the same yesterday, today, and forever (Heb. 13:8).

Not My People? My People!

If we keep this in mind, then what joyous light falls upon Paul's many words about our being children of God. For the story of salvation in the New Testament does not move along a dotted line, with a person saved here and another saved there. In the New Testament we recognize God's rich dealing with His covenant people, as can already be seen in the Old Testament, for He never breaks the relationships built into His creation.

So what did the apostle mean when he wrote that as many as are led by the Spirit of God, these are "sons of God" (Rom. 8:14)? Was he speaking strange words in a foreign language? No! These are not strange words but the old language that sounded familiar to the ears of every Israelite — the language of the covenant. This covenant connection, dating back so many centuries, now becomes the portion of all who were afar off, including those the Lord our God had called at that time and as many as He will call in the future. All the families on earth again came into view. The old word of promise to Abraham had been fulfilled. When in the next chapter the apostle quoted those wonderful words from Hosea, how brightly those words sparkle for those who were afar off, "I will call them My people, who were not My people, and her beloved, who was not beloved. And it shall come to pass in the place where it was said to them, 'You are not My people,' there they shall be called sons of the living God" (Rom. 9:25-26; see Hos. 1:10; 2:22).

Hosea addressed those words to the old covenant people. But the Holy Spirit applies them directly to the situation of the New Day. With these words, all the riches of the old covenant which are fixed in Christ have come to the church of the New Day. The church is called "not of the Jews only, but also of the Gentiles" (Rom. 9:24).

"Not My people" becomes "My people." People! — children belong to a people. Yes, sons! — sons of the living God.

Heirs According to Promise

How rich also are the words we read in the letter to the Galatians in that light, "For you are all sons of God through faith in Christ Jesus" (Gal. 3:26). The "all" refers to all the members of the diverse churches in Galatia (Gal. 1:2). "There is no longer Jew or Greek . . ." (Gal. 3:28). Rather, sonship applies to all, "And if you are Christ's, then you are Abraham's seed, and heirs according to the promise" (Gal. 3:29).

Again, the apostle's words about Abraham's offspring hearken back to the old covenant. The apostle did not do this just for fun or without reason. Nor did he do it in order to make the church of the New Day glad with false hope. Rather, the apostle did this to make them see that God's covenant actually is an "eternal covenant," embracing the old way of "you and your descendants." And if the way of the centuries-long old covenant, with its promise of "you and your descendants," was no longer in effect, Paul would have been obliged to say so clearly.

He did not do this, however. On the contrary, he once again amplified what he had already proclaimed when he said, "then you are Abraham's seed, and *heirs according to the promise*" (Gal. 3:29). What promise? The promise that is discussed throughout Galatians 3, that is, the promise in which God showed His favor to Abraham and "preached the gospel to Abraham beforehand, saying, 'In you all the nations shall be blessed' " (Gal. 3:8). "So then those who are of faith are blessed with believing Abraham" (Gal. 3:9). And this blessing is not for isolated souls, one here and one there, but it is a corporate blessing with Abraham, as his offspring — that is, as his people. There is one people!

With the same purpose, Paul wrote those precious words in his letter to the Ephesians, namely, that the believers who at one time were "without Christ, being aliens from the commonwealth of Israel and strangers from the covenants of promise, having no hope and without God in the world," have now in Christ Jesus been brought near by the blood of Christ. "For He Himself is our peace, who has made both one, and has broken down the middle wall of separation, having abolished in His flesh the enmity, that is, the law of commandments contained in ordinances, so as to create in Himself one new man from the two, thus making peace, and that He might reconcile them both to God in one body through the cross, thereby putting to death the enmity. For through Him we both [Jews and

Gentiles] have access by one Spirit to the Father. Now, therefore, you are no longer *strangers and foreigners, but fellow citizens with the saints and members of the household of God*" (Eph. 2:12-19).

This is in fulfillment of the prophecy of Isaiah, "Do not let the son of the foreigner who has joined himself to the LORD speak, saying, 'The LORD has utterly separated me from His people;' Nor let the eunuch say, 'Here I am, a dry tree.' [For] '. . . Even them I will bring to My holy mountain, and make them joyful in My house of prayer. Their burnt offerings and their sacrifices will be accepted on My altar; For My house shall be called a house of prayer for all nations' " (Isa. 56:3, 7).

In those words "for all nations," we hear the old promise for all the families of the earth. The Lord Jesus' goal was to secure the fulfillment of Isaiah's words. When He cleansed the temple, He didn't try to avoid a clash with the unbelieving leaders of Israel. He looked back to what Isaiah had foretold and He appealed to those words. But He also looked ahead to the future, the future that He was busy preparing in His flesh, the future Paul later spoke about when he said to the Gentiles (and thus also to us) that they are now "being built together for a dwelling place of God in the Spirit" (Eph. 2:22, see 3:1-13). Gentiles are built *together* with God's people. They are the people the apostle says farewell to at the end of his letter to the Galatians with this benediction, "Brethren, the grace of our Lord Jesus Christ be with your spirit" (Gal. 6:18).

They are a people under grace — fathers and mothers with their children, as it was under the old covenant!

Under the Law of Christ

Fathers, mothers, and their children are together also under the law, as was true with the old covenant. This law is the law of Christ. It was written on the heart of their Redeemer, "Behold, I have come . . . to do Your will, O God" (Heb. 10:7). It's the law the Holy Spirit was writing on their hearts, the law of love for God: "We love Him because He first loved us" (1 John 4:19), and the law of love for our neighbor: "He who loves God must love his brother also" (1 John 4:21). This is the law of Christ. "For Christ is the end [the goal] of the law" (Rom. 10:4) — for fathers, for mothers, and for their children. Yes, even for their children.

In 1 Corinthians 1, Scripture reckons the children of believers as "sanctified in Christ Jesus, called to be saints" (1 Cor. 1:2; see 7:14). In the letters to the Ephesians and Colossians, these children are directly addressed, not as outsiders to whom a few scant words come by happenstance, but as those who are fellow citizens and members of the household of God (Eph. 2:19). As we read, "Children, obey your parents in all things, for this is well pleasing to the Lord" (Col. 3:20). The phrase "to the Lord" means the Lord is delighted to receive such obedience from His children. In another place we read, "Honor your father and mother . . . that it may be well with you and you may live long on the earth" (Eph. 6:2-3). Again, this is an address to the children.

Within the circle of God's household, the fathers are mandated to look after their children, "And you, fathers, do not provoke your children to wrath, but bring them up in the training and admonition of the Lord" (Eph. 6:4). We find this same mandate in the old covenant, for Asaph spoke about a law God appointed in Israel, a law "which He commanded our fathers, that they should make them known to their children; that the generation to come might know them . . . that they may set their hope in God" (Ps. 78:5-7).

This is no different than the word of Moses when he addressed all the people, "for God has come to test you, and that His fear may be before you, so that you may not sin" (Ex. 20:20). Neither is this different than God's word to Abraham, "As for you, you shall keep My covenant, you and your descendants after you throughout their generations" (Gen. 17:9). The LORD, who is "I AM," does not change. His covenant is an everlasting covenant.

Grace and law form no contradiction — no light versus darkness. For whoever lives in the light of God's grace, also lives in the light of His law.

> *The law of Your mouth is better to me*
> *Than thousands of coins of gold and silver* (Ps. 119:72).

Blessed Children

Thus God's people are a blessed people. And the children of that people are blessed children. Such was the case under the old covenant. What a blessing to be able to say, "For Thou didst form my inward parts; Thou didst weave me in my mother's womb" (Ps. 139:13, NASB). The psalmist does not say this about a god who is far away but about the LORD who is close to His people in His covenant. David rested in this truth: "You made me trust while on My mother's breasts. I was cast upon You from birth. From My mother's womb You have been My God" (Ps. 22:9b-10).

The poet of Psalm 71 wrote, "By You I have been upheld from birth; You are He who took me out of my mother's womb" (Ps. 71:6). It was because of this blessing that Solomon could say, "Lo, sons are a heritage from the LORD" (Ps. 127:3, RSV). And what a heritage from the LORD, such that we can say with the notes of the old Dutch Bible that children are "a blessing given by the LORD."[6] This blessing of the LORD is not destined for or directed to an eternal grave. If that were the case, David would never have prayed that the sons of Israel might be "as plants grown up in their youth" or that the daughters of Israel might be "as pillars, sculptured in palace style" (Ps. 144:12). For what purpose or to what end would David have covenant children "grown up" or "sculptured"? To be just like the children of the

---

[6] Here the author refers to the marginal notes of the *Statenvertaling,* which is the Dutch translation of the Bible similar to our King James Version. This translation was made by order of the government, i.e., the States General (from which the name of this translation is derived) in accordance with a decree of the Synod of Dort (1618-1619). It was first published in 1637 and included "new explanations of difficult passages and annotations to comparative texts." —TRANS.

uncircumcised, excluded from citizenship in Israel? To be strangers to the covenants of promise? To be without hope, without God and without Christ in the world (Eph. 2:12)?

God won't deal with His people like that (see Ps. 147:20). "For . . . He has blessed your children within you" (Ps. 147:13b). These are the children He commanded to be circumcised and for whom He commanded a lamb (or dove) to be offered as a sacrament of Jesus Christ, the children whom He called with the tender name, "My children" (see Ezek. 16:20-21).

*   *   *

If that is how it was under the old covenant, how would it be under the new covenant? Listen — "Then they brought little children to Him, that He might touch them; but the disciples rebuked those who brought them. But when Jesus saw it, He was greatly displeased and said to them, 'Let the little children come to Me, and do not forbid them; for of such is the kingdom of God' . . . . And He took them up in His arms, put His hands on them, and blessed them" (Mark 10:13-14, 16).

Do we comprehend what was happening here? Do we see in this incident how the Lord Jesus, our Mediator, the one in whom God secured His covenant, traced the line of the covenant (see Heb. 8:6; 9:15; 12:24)?

Christ's feet stood on the foundation of the old dispensation. He did not budge from this foundation, "Do not think that I came to destroy the Law or the Prophets [the Old Testament]. I did not come to destroy but to *fulfill*" (Matt. 5:17). His eyes were fixed on the new covenant in His blood, which would be poured out for many for the remission of sins (Matt. 26:28). And at this turning point in God's redemptive time line, the Lord Jesus kept a tight grip on the children — even the little children. Why? Because He was such a nice man? Because He was a lovely Jesus, a friend of children?

Don't think of Him like that, for we also know Him in a different way. We know Him as He showed Himself to a Greek mother from Syrian Phoenicia (Matt. 15:21-28; Mark 7:24-30). She had a child, too — a little daughter. She brought her to the Lord Jesus, for her daughter was terribly tormented by a demon. That mother begged Him to help. But He gave her no reply. Not a single word! When she persisted, the disciples interjected, "Send her away, for she cries out after us" (Matt. 15:23). The Lord Jesus' reply to them is instructive. He answered, "I was not sent except to the lost sheep of the house of Israel" (v. 24).

In that familiar phrase, "house of Israel," we find the explanation for His behavior toward this mother. The house of Israel denotes the people of God's covenant (see Ps. 98:3; 115:12; Isa. 5:7). A Gentile doesn't belong to God's people and neither does her child. Only when the mother persisted and said, "Lord, help me," did Jesus respond to her. But what a response! He said, "It is not good to take the children's bread and throw it to the little dogs" (v. 26). Dogs! How deeply those words must have cut! If we had been standing in her shoes, wouldn't we have stormed off angrily? But this mother showed great faith (thanks to the Holy Spirit's work) and replied, "Yes, Lord, yet even the little dogs eat the crumbs which fall from their masters' table" (v. 27). So Jesus said, " 'O woman, great is your faith! Let it be to you as you desire.' And her daughter was healed from that very hour" (v. 28). Her faith saved her child.

Certainly in this we see glimmerings of the coming fulfillment of the Abrahamic promise concerning all the families of the earth. Certainly the light of the New Day dawned here, that whoever calls upon the name of the LORD shall be saved (Acts 2:21). Indeed, the light broke through completely after the baptism of Cornelius. Then the apostles and the brothers in Judea glorified God with these words, "Then God has also granted to the Gentiles repentance to life" (Acts 11:18).

But this does not in any way diminish the harsh word the Lord Jesus spoke to that Gentile mother, as one who was outside of Israel — *dogs!* In that word He made a clear distinction between children who were near and Gentiles who were afar off (Eph. 2:13, 17).

In Mark 10, however, we come upon another incident. This time the Lord Jesus was not on Gentile turf, but in Judea. He stood among the people of Abraham. When the disciples rebuked, not a Gentile mother, but mothers of Israel's children, the Lord Jesus was greatly displeased — just as His Father was greatly displeased when Israel brought their sons and daughters as sacrifices to idols (Ezek. 16:20-21). He taught His disciples, who called Him Teacher and Lord — and rightly so, since He is (John 13:13) — how God's way of salvation would progress in the future. He didn't speak impulsively but along the lines of the old covenant.

He showed that in the new dispensation His Father would not release His grip on the family unit. He is faithful. Therefore the Lord Jesus told the disciples, "Let the little children come to Me, and do not forbid them; for of such is the kingdom of God" (Mark 10:14). In other words, don't shut them out of the kingdom of God, for it is not the will of My Father that one of these little ones should perish. Covenant children belong to the kingdom (Luke 13:28). And the disciples needed to know and recognize the Father as "I Am," who is the same yesterday and today, eternally faithful (Heb. 13:8).

So the Lord Jesus "took them [the little children] up in His arms, put His hands on them, and blessed them" (Mark 10:16, see 9:36). That wasn't an empty gesture, suspended meaninglessly in mid-air. What He did was rooted deeply in God's promise to Abraham — the promise to be a God to you and your descendants. Such children are blessed children.

The instruction evidently made a deep impression on the disciples, so deep that when Peter in his Pentecost sermon proclaimed the promise of the Holy Spirit to the "men of Israel," exhorting them to be baptized in the name of the Lord Jesus, he followed in the footsteps of his Lord and immediately involved the children, "*For* the promise is to you and to your children . . ." (Acts 2:39). Such children are blessed children.

*   *   *

And later on, would even one of the apostles be so bold as to point to a different way? Consider Luke. When he describes how the church at Tyre said farewell to the apostle Paul, he tells us that "they all accompanied us, with wives *and children*, till we were out

of the city. And we knelt down on the shore and prayed . . ."
(Acts 21:5) — the children, too.

*   *   *

We have already noted how the apostles included the children
when they addressed the churches. Was this by accident? Did they
do this without reflection? No! Rather, they did this because the
children belonged to and were part of the church. Hence, when Paul
gives his benediction to "the church of God which is at Corinth, to
those who are sanctified in Christ Jesus, called to be saints," using
the words, "Grace to you and peace from God our Father and the
Lord Jesus Christ," he is fully aware of what he is saying and to
whom he is saying it. The blessing applies to the entire congregation.
He will not hinder the children (1 Cor. 1:2-3; 7:14), for such children
are blessed children.

So when we sit in church today and the benediction is
pronounced, that blessing applies to the entire congregation — and
nothing less than that. "The grace of the Lord Jesus Christ, and the
love of God, and the communion of the Holy Spirit be with you all"
(2 Cor. 13:14). Notice that — "you all."

When we were children, we were not excluded from the worship
service, even though we didn't understand all the elements of the
liturgy. Likewise, today, children of the church aren't excluded, for
they aren't afar off. They are near. The blessed congregation includes
its blessed children!

Chapter Seven
A NEW SIGN

In His life and death, the Lord Jesus fulfilled all things (Luke 12:50; John 19:30). He confirmed the promise which was made to the fathers (Rom. 15:8). And God fulfilled that promise by raising Him from the dead (Acts 13:32-33). Only then did He appear in His majesty to the eleven disciples in Galilee where He spoke those powerful words, "All authority has been given to Me in heaven and on earth" (Matt. 28:18).

The Door of Baptism

Such is the situation from this time forward. The Lord Jesus has been given all authority! And since that is true, He properly issues the marching orders for His church: "Go therefore and make disciples of all the nations, *baptizing* them in the name of the Father and of the Son and of the Holy Spirit" (Matt. 28:19).

The Great Commission isn't a careless phrase or an empty command. The Lord Jesus stood on the foundation of God's eternal covenant when He said, "Do not think that I came to destroy the Law or the Prophets. I did not come to destroy but to fulfill" (Matt. 5:17). He stood on that foundation when He took the little children in His arms and blessed them, for the kingdom of heaven belongs to such children (Luke 18:16). He stood on it when, at the Last Supper, He announced the end of Passover lambs and the blood that flowed from them, as He proclaimed the new covenant in His blood (Matt. 26:28). And He continued to stand on that covenant foundation when He uttered the Great Commission, which includes the mandate that all nations be baptized.

All nations! Those words have the familiar ring of a familiar promise — the promise to Abraham that would bring blessing for all the families of the earth (Gen. 12:3). The Abrahamic promise would now be gloriously fulfilled. From East and West the Lord would gather the sheep which He feeds by His hand. And they would sit down with Abraham, Isaac, and Jacob (recipients of the old covenant) in the kingdom of heaven (as recipients of the new covenant) (Matt. 8:11).

And how shall they enter into that glorious reign? Through *baptism!* As in the old dispensation, Israelites (and occasionally aliens, too) were incorporated into the people of God through the door of circumcision (Ex. 12:48), so now in the new dispensation the nations enter the church of the living God *through the door of baptism.*

After the Great Commission, it was only a matter of days till the moment arrived when three thousand souls from the house of Israel entered through that door in a single day (Acts 2:41). Not long after that, an Ethiopian eunuch, a court official of Candace, queen of the Ethiopians, entered in as well (Acts 8:27, 38). Cornelius, the Roman commander, followed (Acts 10:48). And the apostles and brothers in Judea move forward, too. They came so far that they glorified God with these words, "Well then, God has granted to the Gentiles also the repentance that leads to life" (Acts 11:18). *To the Gentiles also!* So the Scripture is fulfilled:

> *I shall mention Rahab and Babylon*
> *Among those who know Me;*
> *Behold, Philistia and Tyre with Ethiopia:*
> *"This one was born there"* (Ps. 87:4).

They entered through the door of hope, the door of baptism.

A Strange Sign?

The baptism Christ institutes is a new sign. Is it also a strange sign? Is it a sign Israel can comprehend only with difficulty?

Absolutely not! We must keep in mind that centuries of divine instruction precede the Lord Jesus instituting the sacrament of baptism.

Like all her neighbors, Israel was not unfamiliar with using water as a common cleansing agent. But more than that, in Scripture we often read that water had a ceremonial purpose. There was ceremonial washing, bathing, and sprinkling. The purpose was not physical hygiene as such, but spiritual purification, to be purified to meet God, consecrated for public worship in the tabernacle or the temple. Thus, when the LORD descended on Mount Sinai, the people had to consecrate themselves and *wash* their clothes (Ex. 19:10, 14).

Before the Levites were permitted to enter into the service of the LORD, they had to be sprinkled with the water of purification (Num. 8:7). Before Aaron and his sons could be ordained to the priesthood, they had to be *washed* (Lev. 8:6). And as often as they entered the tabernacle and brought an offering there, they had to *wash* their hands "lest they die" (Ex. 30:20).

Lepers were not allowed to live among God's people or enter into the house of God. Why? Because they were defiled with death — and God is the God of life! By forbidding lepers from living among His people or entering into His place of worship, the LORD wanted to teach His people that there is no place for death in His presence; thus, no place for the death which lepers carried, so to speak, within their bodies.

Sometimes a leper would get better. Was his uncleanness then simply canceled? Could he now appear again in the fellowship of God's people and before God's face? No, he could not! First he had to go to the priest. Once the priest judged that he was really healed, then he had to be sprinkled with fresh *water*. He had to *bathe* and *wash* his clothes. And then seven days later he again had to bathe and again wash his clothes. Only then could he appear at the tent of meeting. He had to bring the required offerings there, which included a guilt offering, a burnt offering, and a grain offering. "And he shall be clean" (Lev. 14:1-31).

Israel was familiar with the *water of purification*. Numbers 19 contains a detailed description of how this water was to be prepared and how it was to be used. Sometimes an Israelite came into contact with something dead; it was unavoidable — as when a person's father died, or mother or child or spouse. Sometimes a person would come upon a dead body when he entered a tent. Then there was, of course, burial. A person became unclean in all such circumstances. As with lepers, people that had contact with the dead now carried death on themselves and had to be purified.

How was this purification done? As follows: In the course of a week, the unclean person had to be washed twice with the purification water, on the third and seventh days. A ceremonially clean person had to dip a "brush," made from the hyssop plant, into the *water of* purification[7] and then sprinkle it on the unclean person. Then the unclean person had to *wash* his clothes and *bathe* himself. Only then did the unclean person become ceremonially clean again.

The Levitical law stipulated various sorts of ceremonial washings and bathings, all of which were necessary for a person to remain ceremonially clean. Leviticus 15 gives instructions about purification as it pertained to bodily functions and marital intimacy.

*   *   *

Thus for centuries Israel used water as a sign of purification before the LORD. Israel also learned by the water of purification that she should not focus her attention on the outward appearance of the sign. We see this in the Psalms and the Prophets. Because of his sin with Bathsheba, David knew he was completely unclean. Thus in Psalm 51 he prayed:

> *Wash me thoroughly from my iniquity,*
> *And cleanse me from my sin* (v. 2).

And somewhat later:

> *Purge me with hyssop, and I shall be clean;*
> *Wash me, and I shall be whiter than snow* (v. 7).

---

[7] The water of purification consisted of a concoction of ashes — taken from a burned purification offering (cf. Num. 19:2-9; Lev. 14:4 ff) — and fresh (i.e., spring) water. A bundle of hyssop was dipped in the liquid and then used to sprinkle it over the recipient. —TRANS.

With these words David must have remembered the water of purification which is explained in Leviticus 14 and Numbers 19. But then being clean is not limited to purification for worship or purification to enter the forecourt of the tabernacle. No, for what concerned David was his heart:

> *Create in me a clean heart, O God,*
> *And renew a steadfast spirit within me* (v. 10).

Thus in addressing Israel's ungodly leaders, Isaiah said, "Wash yourselves, make yourselves clean; Put away the evil of your doings from before My eyes. Cease to do evil, learn to do good" (Isa. 1:16-17a). Here again we see the symbol of washing, and again it is a matter of the heart, of the cleansing of life. Jeremiah warned, "O Jerusalem, *wash* your heart from wickedness" (Jer. 4:14). And when the LORD, through His prophet Ezekiel, spoke to comfort His people in exile and assured them that He would bring them back to the promised land, He said, "Then I will sprinkle clean water on you, and you shall be clean; I will cleanse you from all your filthiness and from all your idols. I will give you a new heart and put a new spirit within you; I will take the heart of stone out of your flesh and give you a heart of flesh. I will put My Spirit within you and cause you to walk in My statutes, and you will keep My judgments and do them" (Ezek. 36:25-27).

Truly God's people knew for themselves how deeply the metaphor of water, as a sign of inner cleansing, entered into their hearts. Surely they knew that for themselves. The LORD took Israel as His bride. Ezekiel spoke about that also; and here too he used the symbol of *washing* and of *water.* How did this symbol come about for Israel? Where did it come from? How did she become God's bride?

The LORD told her, "Your father was an Amorite and your mother a Hittite" (Ezek. 16:3) — both heathens! And what was Israel as the child of these parents? A neglected child of heathendom. When "you were born, your navel cord was not cut, nor were you *washed* in water to cleanse you" (Ezek. 16:4). Then the LORD passed by and saw her as that little infant lying there. He pitied her. "Then I washed you in water; yes, I thoroughly washed off your blood . . ." (Ezek. 16:9). "Yes, I swore an oath to you and entered into a covenant with you, and you became Mine" (Ezek. 16:8).

Thus we learn that Israel became the LORD's bride *through water.*

* * *

We are familiar with the word "proselyte" from Scripture. A proselyte was a Gentile convert to the Lord (see Acts 2:10; 6:5; 13:43). If a Gentile wanted to be incorporated into the people of Israel, he had to submit to various ceremonies, among them circumcision. But even more, he also had to be *baptized.* Due to the divine instruction about the ceremonial significance of *water* and *washing* from the Old Testament, Israel customarily *used water* in connection with incorporating Gentile converts into God's people.

John — the Preparer of the Way

Thus we see how, in the old dispensation and its old signs, the LORD was already working toward the new dispensation and its new signs. Accordingly, John the Baptist could appear as the "way-preparer" for the Lord (Matt. 3:3). He prepared the way through his preaching which pointed toward his baptism. The entire content of his proclamation was summed up in the sign of baptism, "a baptism of repentance for the remission of sins" (Mark 1:4).

There was no "innovation" in his preaching, for he preached in the spirit and power of Elijah and all the prophets of the old covenant (Luke 1:17). The baptism practiced by John sprang from the repeated old covenant instruction about ceremonial washings, bathings, and sprinklings. In his preaching, John pointed away from himself to Christ. He did this precisely when he spoke about baptism, for he pointed away from his baptism and toward the baptism Christ would institute: "I indeed baptize you with water; but One mightier than I is coming, whose sandal strap I am not worthy to loose. He will baptize you with the Holy Spirit and fire" (Luke 3:16).

John the Baptist was certainly a great prophet. As Jesus said, "Yes, I say to you, and more than a prophet. For this is he of whom it is written: 'Behold, I send My messenger before Your face, who will prepare Your way before You.' Assuredly, I say to you, among those born of women there has not risen one greater than John the Baptist" (Matt. 11:9-11). And John's baptism was a great sign (as circumcision was a great sign), a sign of God's mercy — a sign that had yet to be sealed through the blood of Christ.

But as great as John was, Jesus Christ is greater and stronger. And thus the sign of the baptism which Christ instituted is also greater and stronger than the baptism of John. It too is a sign of God's mercy, but now a mercy secured and permanently sealed in the blood of Christ when He said, "It is finished" (John 19:30). Yes, it is finished once and for all (Heb. 10:14).

Therefore the least in the kingdom of heaven is greater than John the Baptist (Matt. 11:11), for the eyes of the least are able to see what John never saw: "The blind see and the lame walk; the lepers are cleansed and the deaf hear; the dead are raised up and the poor have the gospel preached to them" (Matt. 11:5).

Whoever has seen Christ in this way has seen the Father. And the least in the kingdom of heaven, who receives the baptism of Christ, receives the sign that he is reconciled with the Father through the death of His Son.

Chapter Eight
THE LANGUAGE OF THE NEW SIGN

In Chapter Three we heard the language of the old sign of circumcision. In this chapter we will listen to the language of the new sign of baptism, that is, the baptism that Christ instituted and that Paul called "the circumcision of Christ" (Col. 2:11). Did Paul say this carelessly? Who would dare think that? Paul knew very well what he was writing. When he called baptism "the circumcision of Christ," he knew he stood in the line of God's covenant dispensations.

A Mark of Sin

What is the first thing that baptism teaches us? It teaches that we must be washed. Why? Because we are unclean.

> Behold, I was brought forth in iniquity,
> And in sin my mother conceived me (Ps. 51:5).

That applies to all of us: to young people and to old people, to law-abiding citizens and to criminals.

> There is none righteous, no not one;
> There is none who understands;
> There is none who seeks after God.
> They have all turned aside;
> They have together become unprofitable;
> There is none who does good, no not one (Rom. 3:10-12).

Every mouth is stopped. Before God, the whole world is worthy of damnation (see Rom. 3:19).

So, from where do we know our misery? From our baptism. When we properly see our baptism, our blinders come off. Sin's beautiful shine loses its attraction. Our misery is exposed: our throats are open graves, our tongues practice deceit, the poison of asps is under our lips, our mouth is full of cursing and bitterness, our feet are swift to shed blood, destruction and misery are in our ways, we have not known the way of peace, there is no fear of God before our eyes (Rom. 3:13-18), and the inclination of our carnal mind (that is, our sinful existence) is enmity toward God (Rom. 8:7).

Thus the church does not exaggerate when it confesses, "I am inclined by nature to *hate* God and my neighbor" (*Heidelberg Catechism,* Answer 5). I am *inclined* — that is to say, my entire life leans in the direction of such hatred, like a tree that has grown crooked and leans in the most prominent direction of the wind. To be sure, *hate* is a hateful word. An unbeliever is taken aback by it and says, "Come, come, does humanity's shortcomings have to be expressed so pessimistically?"

Whoever is baptized, however, affirms that word, since it is true. I am totally depraved. And a believer does not need to look at someone else who might be worse. No, for he stands beside the tax collector in the parable. The tax collector did not dare get too close to holy things. He stood afar off and would not raise his eyes to heaven. He beat his breast and said, "God, be merciful to me, a sinner" (Luke 18:9-14). As with circumcision, the first word of baptism is an unmasking (exposing) word (see pages 26-27).

A Mark of Reconciliation

But, fortunately, the first word of baptism is not the last. For the sign of baptism certainly shames us but not without comfort. It does not leave us wallowing in the misery of sin.

Under the old covenant, the sign of circumcision did not do this either; neither did the signs of washings and sprinklings with the water of purification, nor John's baptism. Likewise (under the new covenant) the baptism Christ instituted does not do this, for this baptism *sign*ifies washing and forgiveness. It *sign*ifies the full atonement for all our sins:[8] our evil thoughts, adultery, theft, murder, and divorce, as well as our covetousness, wickedness, deceit, our evil eye and blasphemy, our pride and foolishness. All of these sins grow up like poisonous plants from the swamp of our hearts (Mark 7:21-22). Baptism *sign*ifies nothing less than the end of our misery, the end of the death in which we find ourselves.[9]

Once again, an unbeliever is taken aback by this: "You mean, I'll have to live by atonement? Never!" But whoever has an ear to hear and a heart to understand rejoices in the sign of his baptism. He rejoices in the sign of baptism because, unlike circumcision, it does not call out for better blood, for in the new covenant the water of baptism is the sign of cleansing. As surely as I have been washed with the water of baptism, so certainly my soul is washed from all my impurity through the blood and Spirit of the Lamb of God who takes away the sin of the world (*Heidelberg Catechism*, Answer 69; see John 1:29). That Lamb — without blemish or spot   through one offering, has perfected forever those who are sanctified (1 Pet. 1:19; Heb. 10:14). And this is no human invention. The church fathers, or some ecclesiastical assemblies, didn't make it up. Rather, Scripture speaks this way about baptism. And it does so in more than one place.

*   *   *

Hence, the Lord directed and brought Ananias to Paul. Paul, who had been on his way to Damascus like an unbridled horse, was tamed by the Lord Jesus (see Acts 9:1-19). And what did Ananias say to Paul? The apostle tells us in Acts 22, "Arise and be baptized, and *wash away your sins . . .*" (Acts 22:16). Speaking in an abbreviated manner, Ananias here calls baptism the washing away of sins.

---

[8] See "Form For the Baptism of Infants," *Book of Praise: Anglo-Genevan Psalter*, p. 584.

[9] See "Form For the Celebration of the Lord's Supper," *Book of Praise: Anglo-Genevan Psalter*, p. 594.

Does that then mean you can wash away sins with water? Ananias certainly knew better than that. And Paul, who knew the old covenant Scriptures, certainly knew better as well. But as the Lord Jesus could say in the institution of the Lord's Supper: this is My body, and of the cup: this is My blood of the new covenant (Matt. 26:26, 28), so Ananias can say here: baptism is the *washing away of sins.* This is not a careless statement spoken independently of Christ. Rather, to those words Ananias added the phrase, "calling on the name of the Lord [i.e. Christ]" (Acts 22:16).

*   *   *

We find the same abbreviated, pointed language about baptism in Paul's first epistle to the Corinthians. In that letter Paul wrote about wrongdoers: "fornicators, idolaters, adulterers, homosexuals, sodomites, thieves, covetous, drunkards, revilers, extortioners." Such do not "inherit the kingdom of God" (1 Cor. 6:9-10). "And such," Paul said, "were some of you. But you were *washed . . .*" (1 Cor. 6:11).

This is a clear and unmistakable reminder of baptism — again, in abbreviated language. *Washed.* How? By baptism? Indeed. But baptism as understood in light of the entire witness of Scripture, for Paul continues, "you were sanctified, you were justified . . ." (1 Cor. 6:11). Sanctified and justified — how? By the water of baptism in itself? No. Rather, as we read on, "in the name of the Lord Jesus and by the Spirit of our God" (1 Cor. 6:11), for to be baptized is to be joined to the Father and to the Son and to the Holy Spirit. As in Christ's institution of baptism all three persons of the Godhead are named, so Paul mentions all three persons here in 1 Corinthians 6:11. Our union with the Father, Son, and Holy Spirit is all here in that one sign — that is, in the baptism instituted by Christ — which, as a sign, makes clear what happens. And as a seal it guarantees that the sign is not empty talk, but reliable truth. Whoever has his or her unrighteousness and impurity washed away in baptism is clean indeed. For the words (and promises) of people can pass away — *there is so little fidelity in the world.* But the word of God's promises and signs is unshakable.

Thus Paul can also tell the believers at Ephesus that Christ has cleansed His church "with the washing of water by the word" (Eph. 5:26). Again we find the same manner of speaking — powerful and to the point.

In Hebrews we read, "Therefore, brethren, having boldness to enter the Holiest by the blood of Jesus, . . . let us draw near with a true heart in full assurance of faith, having our hearts sprinkled from an evil conscience and our bodies washed [in baptism] with pure water" (Heb. 10:19, 22). The apostle Peter speaks no differently when he said that baptism is "not the removal of dirt from the flesh, but an appeal to God for a good conscience . . ." (1 Pet. 3:21, NASB). Note that, an appeal to God!

To accept the baptism of Christ means to look away from yourself. It means to recognize that you lie in the midst of death. And it means to look prayerfully to Jesus who is the only Savior, "for there is no other name under heaven given among men by which we must be saved" (Acts 4:12). To accept baptism is to humble yourself — to humble yourself to the depths of the swamp of your sin. But then like the tax collector, you go forth justified (see pages 27-28). For whoever humbles himself will be exalted (Luke 18:14). That is the very same message as that of circumcision.

As far as the east is from the west,
So far has He removed our transgressions from us (Ps. 103:12).

A Mark of New Life

We have not yet exhausted the significance of the sign of baptism.

Titus labored in the church on the island of Crete. He exhorted both young and old, men, women, and slaves, that "they may adorn the doctrine of God our Savior in all things" (Titus 2:10). He reminded them how they used to live: "foolish, disobedient, deceived, serving various lusts and pleasures, living in malice and envy, hateful and hating one another" (Titus 3:3). "But," wrote Paul, "when the kindness and the love of God our Savior toward man appeared, . . . He saved us, through the washing of regeneration and renewing of the Holy Spirit" (Titus 3:4-5).

Regeneration and renewal. Israel had already learned about that through the sign of circumcision (see pages 28-29). David knew about it:

> *Create in me a clean heart, O God,*
> *And renew a steadfast spirit within me* (Ps. 51:10).

The Lord Jesus impressed the same thing upon Nicodemus, "Truly, truly, I say to you, unless one is born again, he cannot see the kingdom of God" (John 3:3, NASB; also 3:5). Paul wrote the same thing to Titus: we must be born again; our lives must be renewed. How? By one's own effort? By our own strength? No. Rather, by *washing* — the washing of regeneration and renewal, the washing of baptism.

So, does that mean we are reborn by a little water? No, for all the water in the ocean cannot wash away our sins. We know better. After all, in connection with the teaching in Titus about the washing of regeneration and renewal, we also find the Holy Spirit mentioned. He alone regenerates and renews. And that washing, that water, is nothing more than the sign and the guarantee of what Christ desires to do and is doing in us through the Holy Spirit. Baptism is nothing more than that.

But nothing less, either — for Christ Himself instituted baptism. And He makes no empty gestures. He baptizes with the Holy Spirit and with fire (Matt. 3:11). Consequently, we must not minimize the washing of baptism, for it is a great event. Whoever is baptized in Christ is joined to Christ for good. He has become a new creation; the old has passed away. See, the miracle of the new has come (2 Cor. 5:17). This miracle is the "resurrection from the dead, [the] making alive, so highly spoken of in the Scriptures, which God works in us without us" (*Canons of Dort,* 3/4, 12).

The unspiritual person, who is not led by the Spirit of God, does not accept this. He cannot understand it because it is spiritually (that is, Spiritually) discerned (1 Cor. 2:14). But the spiritual person knows it is true, even though he does not know how rebirth takes place. "It is, however, clearly a supernatural, most powerful, and at the same time most delightful, marvelous, mysterious, and inexpressible work . . ." (*Canons of Dort,* 3/4, 12).

*   *   *

Our new life, which came about without our knowledge, must sprout. The spring sunshine of God's grace produces the freshness of new life. In this process the Lord does not treat us as if we were stocks and blocks. Rebirth does not occur without our awareness (*Canons of Dort*, 3/4, 16). That is why the clarion sounds in the Scriptures, "Awake, you who sleep, arise from the dead . . ." (Eph. 5:14). Arise! Arise from the dead! Arise to new life! Not that we have already obtained it or that we have already been perfected (Phil. 3:12). No, no! — "I find then a law, that evil is present with me, the one who wills to do good" (Rom. 7.21). But the washing of regeneration and renewal teaches us, and guarantees to us, that "we are being transformed [from day to day] into the same image from glory to glory, just as by the Spirit of the Lord" (2 Cor. 3:18). For Christ baptizes with the Holy Spirit and with fire.

The Holy Spirit makes our unwilling hearts willing to live for God. He heals our sinful will and causes it to bow to the will of God — "pleasantly and at the same time powerfully" (*Canons of Dort,* 3/4, 16). He refines us with fire, as silver is refined (Ps. 66:10), so that with our spirits on fire we serve the Lord and present ourselves as living, holy sacrifices to Him (Rom. 12:1, 11).

Thus baptism is the washing of regeneration and renewal leading to our putting off (like a piece of clothing) the deeds of darkness and our putting on (like a suit of armor or a battle garment) the armor of light (Col. 3:9-10; Rom. 13:12). This washing means putting on the new man, which is created according to the will of God in true righteousness and holiness (Eph. 4:24). In a word, it is putting on the Lord Jesus Christ (again, like a garment) in complete solidarity with Him (Rom. 13:14).

For this reason, we who are baptized can no longer live in sin. To be sure, we can fall into sin. We can also fall into the same sin more than once. We can even, perhaps, struggle with the same sin our whole life long, with the consequence that we become discouraged at times. But we cannot live in sin. We cannot thrive in sin. We cannot find our happiness in sin, for "whoever abides in Him does not sin" (1 John 3:6). The Scriptures speak about this very strongly in Romans 6 (which is a chapter about baptism). And in this chapter Paul relates baptism to two things: to the death of Christ and to the resurrection (or the life) of Christ.

Our baptism is a baptism into the death of Christ, that is, it is a death-bed baptism, a baptism of burial (Rom. 6:3-4). Paul says that "we have been planted together with Christ in the likeness of His death." That is how the King James Version translates it.[10] The New King James Version translates that phrase this way, "we have been united together in the likeness of His death" (Rom. 6:5).[11] We have grown into Christ in baptism just as a twig grows into the branch to which it is grafted. From then on, the twig receives everything from the branch — sap, nourishment, fruitfulness.

That is how tightly and closely we are joined to Christ in His death. We have died with Him (Rom. 6:8). When did this happen? It happened when He was crucified (Rom. 6:6). Thus we died. We died to sin (Rom. 6:11). And what were we before this death? We were slaves to sin, wholly under its power. Sin had a claim on us and was our master (Rom. 6:20). Now that we have died to sin, however, we are set free; we are legally free from sin. It can no longer assert its claims over us. Sin has nothing more to say to us (Rom. 6:7).

---

[10] Here the author refers to the *Statenvertaling*, which has the translation, "We have become one plant with Christ in the likeness of his death." —TRANS.

[11] The author here is referring to a new Dutch translation by the *Nederlands Bijbelgenootschap*. More recent English versions provide a similar translation. —TRANS.

This is what Romans 6 shows us, on the one hand. But because we have been united to Christ in baptism, we also receive the fruits of His death. These fruits are reconciliation by His blood and renewal by His Spirit — for our baptism is not only a baptism into Christ's death, it is also a baptism into Christ's resurrection. "For if we have been united together in the likeness of His death [if we have become one plant with Him], certainly we also shall be in the likeness of His resurrection" (Rom. 6:5; also see Col. 2:12-13).

When does this happen? Will it take place later, perhaps? Will it take place after judgment day, on the new earth? Yes, it will take place completely then and there, to be sure. But this is not what the apostle is discussing in Romans 6, for he is dealing with the present, a resurrection in this life, on this earth. As the Scriptures say, ". . . reckon yourselves to be dead indeed to sin [already here and now], but alive to God in Christ Jesus our Lord" (Rom. 6:11). Must we consider ourselves in this state because, here and now, we are doing so well, because we are making such nice progress day by day?

No, for the apostle also has written, "I find then a law, that evil is present with me, the one who wills to do good" (Rom. 7:21). Don't we experience this truth every day? Don't young and old alike experience this — that sin is still so strong in us? So invincible? "O wretched man that I am! Who will deliver me from this body of death" (Rom. 7:24)?

Are not then the wonderful words of Romans 6 — "reckon yourselves to be dead indeed to sin, but alive to God" — an exaggeration, simply too far beyond our reach? No, for it is the same author in the same letter who in one and the same connection wrote both of these things. Moreover, it is the same Spirit of Christ who governed Paul's pen in both Romans 6 and Romans 7.

Thus, don't be discouraged in reading Romans 6. Don't be afraid that you are not united to the Lord Jesus because the words "to be dead indeed to sin, but alive to God" don't seem applicable to you. Don't think that a lot has to happen to you before you may validly say that your old self has been crucified with Christ. Don't fear that baptism is thus invalid for you, for surely it is valid. It is valid for you. It is valid for me. And it is valid for anyone who receives Christ, for just read carefully the words that follow, "Now if we died with Christ [through baptism!], we believe that we shall also live with Him" (Rom. 6:8). That's what we believe. Not that we have already obtained it, or have already become perfect. But in faith we say, ". . . I press on, that I may lay hold of that" (Phil. 3:12). And we don't press on because we are so persistent, but because "Christ Jesus has also laid hold of me" (Phil. 3:12).

Yes, "For the death that He died, He died to sin once for all; but the life that He lives, He lives to God" (Rom. 6:10). How does Christ live to God? By idly doing nothing? No! Rather, as the Head of His church, His fullness fills all in all (Eph. 1:23). He takes hold of sinners every day (and makes them His own) that they may live for God, for sin shall not have dominion over us (Rom. 6:14a). That's not big talk. That's not even a command. Rather, it is a promise! — "for you are not under law but under grace" (Rom. 6:14b). Who will rescue us from this body of death? "I thank God — through Jesus Christ our Lord!" (Rom. 7:25).

A Mark of God's People

As with the language of circumcision, we can summarize the language of baptism in one word: *incorporation* (see page 29). Those who are baptized are incorporated into the church of the living God, into the church of Christ (1 Tim. 3:15; Gal. 1:22). This is the church that has held Christ before her eyes from the beginning, "And I . . . say to you that you are Peter, and on this rock I will build My church . . ." (Matt. 16:18); it is the church that is called His body, "Now you are the body of Christ and individually members of it" (1 Cor. 12:27); it is the church that is named the *house of God*, "because," as it is expressed so well, "God lives in it with His Spirit and Word"[12] (see 1 Tim. 3:15; 2 Cor. 6:16; Heb. 3:6).

---

[12] Quoted from the marginal notes of the *Statenvertaling*.

We are incorporated into this church through baptism, for we are united to Christ through baptism. We become one plant with the one who "loved the church and gave Himself for her, that He might sanctify and cleanse her with the washing of water by the word . . ." (Eph. 5:25-26). We are baptized into this body by the one Spirit (1 Cor. 12:13), just as we were also called to this body in one baptism (Eph. 4:3-5). In that house of God we live as "fellow citizens . . . built on the foundation of the apostles [the new covenant] and prophets [the old covenant], Jesus Christ Himself being the chief Cornerstone" (Eph. 2:19-20). And we live there as children, "For you are all sons of God through faith in Christ Jesus. For as many of you as were baptized into Christ have put on Christ" (Gal. 3:26-27).

The Seal

Thus we see that the language of baptism is the same as that of circumcision. Baptism is even, as with circumcision, a *seal*. It's a guarantee (see page 29 30). Just as the sign of the rainbow is a guarantee that God will never again destroy the whole world with a flood, so the sign of baptism is a guarantee that sin will no longer have dominion over us (Gen. 9:8-17; Rom. 6:9). There are more examples like this. Just as the sign of circumcision was a seal and guarantee of the righteousness of faith for Abraham and his descendants, so the sign of baptism is a guarantee that we are justified by faith in Jesus Christ (Rom. 4:11, 24; 5:1). Just as the blood on the doorposts was an assurance that God would spare the firstborn of Israel, so baptism is an assurance that the death and shed blood of Christ are life for us (Ex. 12:13; 2 Cor. 5:14-15). Just as surely as water washes away dirt from our bodies, so certainly are we washed from our sins in baptism (Acts 22:16; Heb. 10:22). Just as surely as through baptism we have become one plant with Christ in His death and resurrection, so certainly have we died to sin and become alive to God with Christ (Rom. 6:5). Just as surely as we are baptized into Christ, so certainly we have been clothed with Him and have become sons and daughters of God, members of His body which is the church (Gal. 3:26-27; 1 Cor. 12:13, 27).

Why is this so? Because our faith is so strong at the moment of baptism? Because our faith remains so strong even when our baptism lies years behind us? Not at all, for daily the Lord must help our unbelief (Mark 9:24). If the power of baptism depended on our faith . . . Oh my! No, baptism as a seal has power, baptism's guarantee is valid, not because we support it with our faith, but because the triune God Himself confers power to baptism as a door of hope. God Himself supports it!

For what does it mean when the Lord Jesus commands His disciples, and with them His church, to baptize the nations in the name of the Father and of the Son and of the Holy Spirit (Matt. 28:19)? In order to prevent misunderstanding, let us first establish that it does not mean: baptize *on behalf of* the Father and the Son and the Holy Spirit. Nor does it mean: baptize *by order of* the Father and the Son and the Holy Spirit.

So what does it mean? It means that through baptism we are closely and permanently united to the Father and to the Son and to the Holy Spirit.[13] Whoever is baptized, henceforward belongs to God. From that moment onward we are in God's care. We come under the care of the Father and of the Son and of the Holy Spirit — the Father who establishes an everlasting covenant with us and accepts us as His children and heirs; the Son with whom we have become one plant in His death and resurrection; and the Holy Spirit who has been given to us as surely as Christ died for the ungodly, that is, while we were still without strength (Rom. 5:6), and who wants to live in us and to make us living members of Christ (1 Cor. 12:27). All of this is *absolutely* guaranteed to us in baptism.

*   *   *

But someone might ask where that can be found in the Bible.

---

[13] According to Dr. C. Trimp, Matt. 28:19 can be literally translated "baptizing them *unto* the name of the Father, and of the Son, and of the Holy Spirit." See his *De Gemeente en haar Liturgie* [*The Church and its Liturgy*] (Kampen: Van den Berg, 1983), pp. 193-194. For the same translation Trimp refers to Acts 8:16; 19:5; 1 Cor. 1:13-15; Rom. 6:3; Gal. 3:27; and 1 Cor. 10:2.

We can give Scriptural references for the guarantees to Noah, Abraham, Israel, Gideon, and Hezekiah. But where does the Lord explicitly assure us that baptism is not just a sign but also a seal, a guarantee?

The answer is both simple and certain. This guarantee is offered to us in the *command* of Christ, "Go therefore and make disciples of all the nations, baptizing them in the name of the Father and of the Son and of the Holy Spirit" (Matt. 28:19; see Mark 16:16).

Perhaps someone feels a bit disappointed with this proof text? He asks himself: But is there a single word here that baptism would give us a *certifying seal* or *guarantee*?

Yes! Even a clear word, for if Christ commands us to baptize the nations, then that *command* is as good as His *promise* — a promise in which He does not speak one empty word, not one word without meaning. For we must trust in Jesus Christ, about whom only a bit earlier the Father had said from the cloud, "This is My beloved Son, in whom I am well pleased. Hear Him!" (Matt. 17:5).

In view of the fact that now all authority in heaven and on earth is given to Him, shouldn't we listen to Him when He commands us to baptize the nations? Shouldn't we lean all our weight on this promise, like we lean in weariness against a cabinet or a counter? When He shows the way (which is the way of salvation), must we then ask ourselves whether that might be the wrong way? Do we need a witness more trustworthy than the command of His mouth? And shouldn't what He said about all of His teaching apply to this command: "Therefore whoever hears these sayings of Mine, and does them, I will liken him to a wise man who built his house on the rock: and the rain descended, the floods came, and the winds blew and beat on that house; and it did not fall, for it was founded on the rock" (Matt. 7:24-25)? Moreover, if the Holy Spirit calls baptism "the washing away of sins" and "the washing of regeneration" (Acts 22:16; Titus 3:5), who of us still dares to think that the guarantee of baptism is unstable, something we can never be sure of?

"Therefore, brethren [brothers and sisters], since we have confidence to enter the holy place by the blood of Jesus . . . let us draw near with a sincere heart in full assurance of faith, having our hearts sprinkled *clean* from an evil conscience and our bodies washed [through baptism] with pure water" (Heb. 10:19, 22, NASB; see Rom. 4:11; Gal. 3:6-9, 26-29).

For the *command* of Christ is at the same time His *promise*.

The Circumcision of Christ

We have seen that the sign of circumcision spoke first of all about sin, which is an obstacle that prevents us from coming to God. The sign of baptism speaks of the same thing. The sign of circumcision spoke also about the removing of and atoning for sin. Baptism says this as well. Consequently, circumcision spoke about new life before God — life from the dead. Baptism declares this too. Circumcision was the identifying mark of God's own people, a sign of incorporation into that people. The same holds true for baptism. Circumcision was a seal and guarantee of God's covenant promises. Likewise, baptism is such a seal or guarantee.

*   *   *

Is it strange then that the Bible, specifically in the letter to the Colossians, calls baptism "the circumcision of Christ" (Col. 2:11-12)? How does Paul come up with this?

We know that erroneous teaching was being propagated in the church at Colosse (and perhaps in the church of Laodicea as well, Col. 4:16). What precisely these aberrant teachings were cannot be determined from the letter. But this much we do know: it had to do with knowledge.

Some supposed that they possessed a deep, philosophical knowledge, a knowledge that was deeper than the knowledge of Christ (Col. 2:8). For example, they prided themselves in having been initiated into a realm of knowledge dealing with the angelic world and spiritual powers (Col. 1:16; 2:15). Moreover, they taught that if you wanted to receive such deep knowledge, then you needed to know a few things about this realm. You needed to live in harmony with the first principles of the world, meaning: you had to learn the *A B C*s of the religious (or Jewish) life regarding festivals, new moons, Sabbaths, and the like (Col. 2:16-17). Furthermore, you had to die to yourself — don't eat this and don't drink that; don't handle and don't touch (Col. 2:21). If you persisted in such a way of life, you were on the right track. And if you were originally a Jew, then you were immediately in a favorable position, for then you would have already been circumcised! And you would have had a head start in searching for that deep knowledge — as well as being in an advantageous position with respect to good and evil, angels and spiritual powers, principalities, thrones and dominions in heaven or on earth (Col. 1:16; 2:15).

To be sure, they did not say that Gentile believers had to be circumcised (we don't read anything of that in Colossians). But apparently the Gentile believers were impressed with this knowledge — what knowledge these teachers possessed! What insight! And how religious it all looked! Compared with the superior knowledge of these teachers, didn't their meager faith in Christ look impoverished?

Paul, however, wrote and told them not to lose their heads over sophistry or empty talk that was not in harmony with Christ (Col. 2:4), for in Christ, he assured them, you have received "*all* the wealth that comes from the *full assurance* of understanding *resulting* in a true knowledge of God's mystery . . ." (Col. 2:2, NASB). Indeed, Christ is the Head over all principalities and powers in heaven and on earth.

Thus, when these "deep thinkers" boasted of their circumcision, and believers bumped up against such boasting, then Paul urged them to take heart. "You also were circumcised," he told them (Col. 2:11).

They were circumcised? Ordinary Gentile believers? How could this be? The answer is: Because you have entered death and the grave with Christ, dying to sin when you were "buried with Him in baptism" (Col. 2:12).

Circumcision declared: The body of the flesh must be put off. Apply the knife! Indeed the believers at Colosse had done this very thing: they had put off sin. They did this not with a circumcision performed by human hands, of which the false teachers boasted, but rather, with the circumcision of Christ (Col. 2:11).

And if those boastful teachers asked these timid believers when that happened, there was a ready reply: When I was baptized! — baptized in Christ (Col. 2:12), when I was clothed with Christ (Gal. 3:27), when I became one plant with Christ (Rom. 6:5).

Paul knew the language of circumcision from his youth. Later he became familiar with the language of the baptism of Christ. What did he thus come to understand? This: that both circumcision and baptism, despite the difference that certainly exists, have one and the same meaning. They speak one and the same language.

Is it then any wonder that he calls baptism "the circumcision of Christ"? It is really quite simple and quite clear. "For we are the circumcision, who worship God in the Spirit, rejoice in Christ Jesus, and have no confidence in the flesh" (Phil. 3:3).

As for knowledge, the apostle says that the ordinary believers at Colosse have put off the old man with its practices "and have put on the new man who is renewed (note that!) in *knowledge* according to the image of Him who created him, where there is neither Greek nor Jew, circumcised nor uncircumcised . . . but Christ is all and in all!" (Col. 3:10-11).

Bloody — Bloodless

If, however, circumcision and baptism speak the same language, then the question may be asked why it was necessary for a new sign to take the place of the old one? Why does baptism need to replace circumcision?

We find the answer by asking a few more questions, such as: Why did God tear in half the veil of the temple at the death of His Son (Matt. 27:51), after all, it hung there according to His own prescription (Ex. 26:31-34; Heb. 9:7-12)? Why did the great day of atonement become unnecessary after Christ's death? Wasn't it God who had instituted that day (Lev. 16)? Why did the shedding of the blood of sacrificial animals come to an end after the death of Christ (Heb. 10:2)? Didn't God Himself prescribe in detail the sacrificial service (Lev. 1-7)? Likewise, why was Passover replaced by the Holy Supper after the death of Christ (1 Cor. 10:16-17; 11:23-26), after all, the Father ordained the Passover as a memorial meal and a memorial offering for His own people (Ex. 12:14)?

Don't we all know the answer to these various questions? These things had to change because Christ stands at the turning point of God's dispensations. He is the Lamb of God who takes away the sin of the world (John 1:29). "For it is not possible that the blood of bulls and goats could take away sins" (Heb. 10:4). On a specific day, able to be marked on our calendar, Christ could say, "It is finished!" (John 19:30). He fulfilled the Law and the Prophets to the last jot and tittle (Matt. 5:18). *Fulfilled.* This means He has revealed the full meaning, the full significance of the Law and the Prophets.

Therefore, now [because of the fulfillment] the veil of the temple could be torn in two: the great day of atonement was no longer necessary. Now the ministry surrounding the temple comes to an end. Now the flow of blood from sacrificial animals had to dry up in order to make room for the blood of the new covenant (Matt. 26:28; Ex. 24:8). Now it was also time that the bitter and bloody sign of circumcision, which pointed to and called out for better blood than that of little boys, be replaced by another sign which did not involve the shedding of blood. Now another law appears concerning incorporation into the people of God, for under the old dispensation, the Old Testament, that law was the mandate of circumcision; under the new dispensation, the New Testament, that law is the mandate of Christ: Go therefore and make disciples of all the nations, baptizing them in the name of the Father and of the Son and of the Holy Spirit (Matt. 28:19).

Baptism has become the *circumcision of Christ* (Col. 2:11). Baptism points back to Christ's blood. It teaches us to rest in the blood of the covenant by which we are sanctified (Heb. 10:29).

This was according to God's counsel, appointed beforehand (Acts 3:18; 4:28). When the blood of bulls and goats is no longer necessary, can the call continue to sound forth for the blood of little boys?

Bloody — bloodless. In those two words lies the answer to the question at hand: Why a new sign? The more we see the paramount significance of Christ — that is, see Him as the One who "has become a servant to the circumcision for the truth of God, to confirm the promises made to the fathers, and that the Gentiles might glorify God for His mercy . . ." (Rom. 15:8-9) — the more we will understand that the Law and the Prophets are fulfilled in Him; indeed, everything is fulfilled in Him.

Therefore the old has passed over into the new. The old signs had to be replaced by the new. Meanwhile, in this substitution of the one for the other, the heart of the matter remains eternally the same, namely, God's pity for a fallen world, God's faithfulness to Himself, His eternal good pleasure. He is Yahweh — I AM WHO I AM (Ex. 3:14), the same yesterday, today, and forever (Heb. 13:8).

*   *   *

Our baptism is a sign and a seal. It is a sign of faithfulness, of God's faithfulness.

Chapter Nine
ONE PEOPLE OF GOD

The church. The body of Christ. The house of God. Such are the *people* of God in the new dispensation.

Sometimes one hears talk about God's old covenant people, meaning the Jews. That language might create the impression that there are two separate peoples of God — an old and a new.

God's One Work

Is God's work, then, split up? Is His first building project broken off? Does God have to renew His work in a second project? No, Scripture speaks of one work of divine salvation. There is no crack in His redemptive plan (see pages 33f.).

In Genesis 15 Abraham looked up at the stars, "So shall your descendants be" (Gen. 15:5). In Genesis 17 Abram's name was changed, ". . . your name shall be Abraham; for I have made you a father of *many* nations" (Gen. 17:5). Were these two utterances of the LORD detached and independent of each other? Was Abraham to play a dual role? Was he to become the father of his descendants — namely, the old covenant people — but then alongside and independent of them, was he to be the father of many nations, that is, of a new covenant people?

No. In the letter to the Romans Scripture joins both of these divine utterances together and places them on one level: "[Abraham], contrary to hope, in hope believed, so that he became the father of many nations [Genesis 17], according to what was spoken, 'So shall your descendants be' [Genesis 15]" (Rom. 4:18).

And in Romans 9, Paul again quotes the words of the LORD, this time from the prophecy of Hosea:

> *I will call them My people, who were not My people,*
> *And her beloved, who was not beloved.*
> *And it shall come to pass*
> *In the place where it was said to them,*
> *"You are not My people,"*
> *There they shall be called sons of the living God*
> (Rom. 9:25-26; see Hos. 2:22; 1:10).

So who are those whom Paul by the Spirit calls "My people" and "beloved"? In Romans 9:23 they are called by name, as it were. They are the "vessels of mercy . . . whom He called, not of the Jews only, but also of the Gentiles" (Rom. 9:23-24).

Thus what are we to conclude? This: Scripture uses the same phrase which was originally directed to Israel by Hosea to describe the Gentiles to whom God has been merciful. It was obviously one phrase for God's one people.

*   *   *

Scripture speaks no differently in the second letter to the Corinthians. Paul warns the church not to become unequally yoked with unbelievers, for "what agreement has the temple of God with idols? For you are the temple of the living God. As God has said: 'I will dwell in them and walk among them. I will be their God, and they shall be My people' " (2 Cor. 6:16).

What was the time and place God first said that? It was at Sinai when the LORD gave His laws. And He promised His blessing too: "If you walk in My statutes and keep My commandments, and perform them . . . I will set My tabernacle among you . . . . I will walk among you and be your God, and you shall be My people" (Lev. 26:3, 11-12).

These words were intended for Israel, that is, for the old covenant people. Does that then mean they are not intended for the new covenant people? Surely, they are also intended for them, for God does not have two separate covenant peoples, an old and a new. Neither are there two temples of the living God, an old and a new.

Israel forms this temple, as does the church of Corinth. And we, the believers and churches of the present century, are equally included.

*   *   *

In Romans 11, when Paul used the symbol of the olive tree into which wild branches are grafted, did he talk about two trees, an old and a new? No! It is *one* tree from the *one* root of God's *one* people (Rom. 11:16-24).

God's One People

Let us for a moment take another look at Mount Sinai. There "Moses went up to God, and the LORD called to him from the mountain, saying, 'Thus you shall say to the house of Jacob, and tell the children of Israel . . . "Now therefore, if you will indeed obey My voice and keep My covenant, then you shall be a special treasure to Me above all people; for all the earth is Mine. And you shall be to Me a kingdom of priests and a holy nation." These are the words which you shall speak to the children of Israel' " (Ex. 19:3-6).

Are those words distinctly meant for the old covenant people alone? No! For Scripture teaches something completely different. God has laid "in Zion a chief Cornerstone, elect, precious" — Christ. He was given also for the "old" covenant people. "And he who believes on Him will by no means be put to shame" (1 Pet. 2:6).

But what happened? The builders — that is, Israel in her leaders — rejected this Cornerstone (1 Pet. 2:7). They rejected the Son of God. They did not keep God's covenant but fell away from Him (Matt. 21:33-46).

Therefore their stumbling means riches for the whole world (Rom. 11:11-12). In his first letter, the apostle Peter had written to Gentiles in Pontus, Galatia, Cappadocia, Asia, and Bithynia — Gentiles who had accepted Christ as the precious Cornerstone (1 Pet. 1:1). And Peter addressed them with these words, "But you are a chosen generation, a royal priesthood, a holy nation, His own special people . . ." (1 Pet. 2:9).

Those words are from Exodus 19. They are the very same words for the very same people of God, God's one people.

How could Peter have spoken any differently? He was the one who first confessed, "You are the Christ, the Son of the living God" (Matt. 16:16), the Consolation of Israel (Luke 2:25). He was the one who shortly after this confession witnessed along with James and John that wondrous sight on the holy mountain: Moses and Elijah — *old* covenant — speaking with Christ about His departure, a departure the Lord Jesus would fulfill in Jerusalem to confirm the *new* covenant in His blood (Luke 9:31). Peter was the one who after this earth-shaking event heard the voice from the Excellent Glory, the voice of the eternal God: "This is My beloved Son, in whom I am well pleased" (2 Pet. 1:17). He was the one on the day of Pentecost who, by the Holy Spirit, could trace the line of Moses through David, Elijah, Joel, Hosea, and Christ. "For the promise is to you and to your children, and to all who are afar off, as many as the Lord our God will call" (Acts 2:39). Peter was the one who, like Paul, quoted the words of Hosea:

> *For you once were not a people,*
> *But now you are the people of God;*
> *You had not received mercy,*
> *But now have received mercy* (1 Pet. 2:10, NASB).

God's One Temple

It is very important to see God's ways properly, especially if we are to gain a proper understanding of baptism as a sign of faithfulness, as a sign for us. It is not for nothing that Scripture devotes so much attention to these matters.

*   *   *

Paul did that anew in his letter to the Ephesians. He wrote those believers and told them that they belong to the people God has made His own, to the praise of His glory (Eph. 1:14). Moreover, they belonged even though they were formerly dead in their trespasses and sins (Eph. 2:1). God, however, who is rich in mercy, made them alive together with Christ (Eph. 2:4-5). They were God's workmanship, created in Christ Jesus for good works, so that they

— like Abraham in former times — might walk in them (Eph. 2:10). "Therefore," the apostle continued, "remember that you, once Gentiles in the flesh . . . that at that time you were without Christ, being aliens from the commonwealth of Israel and strangers from the *covenants of promise . . .*" (Eph. 2:11-12).

Thus, such was their situation by birth. They stood outside the covenant, "having no hope and without God in the world. But now in Christ Jesus you who once were far off have been brought near by the blood of Christ. For He Himself is our peace, who has made both one, and has broken down the middle wall of separation [between Jew and Gentile] . . . so as to create in Himself one new man from the two, thus making peace, and that He might reconcile them both to God in one body through the cross, thereby putting to death the enmity. And He came and preached peace to you who were afar off and to those who were near. For through Him we both [Jews and Gentiles] have access by one Spirit to the Father" (Eph. 2:12b-18). So what is their situation now?

*   *   *

Listen, "Now, therefore, you are no longer strangers and foreigners, but fellow citizens with the saints and members of the household of God, having been built on the foundation of the apostles [new covenant] and prophets [old covenant], Jesus Christ Himself being the chief Cornerstone, in whom the whole building, being joined together, grows into a holy temple in the Lord" (Eph. 2:19-21; see 2 Cor. 6:16; 7:1).

In Christ, who is also the Cornerstone, those who were Gentiles by birth, now have become "fellow heirs" and "partakers of His promise in Christ," "in whom you also are being built together for a dwelling place of God in the Spirit," "into a holy temple in the Lord" (Eph. 3:6; 2:19-22).

One People — One Language

God's one work. God's one people. God's one temple. Why? For "I AM WHO I AM" (Ex. 3:14). And "Jesus Christ is the same yesterday and today and forever" (Heb. 13:8).

Thus the magnificent words God used to comfort His people in the Old Testament are not lost in the New Testament — neither the word *people* (as we saw above), nor the beautiful word *covenant,* nor the words *flock* and *shepherd,* and to mention one more, the tender word *bride.*

We will look briefly at each of these terms.

Covenant

In the Old Testament: "And I will establish My *covenant* between Me and you . . . for an everlasting covenant, to be God to you and your descendants after you" (Gen. 17:7). " 'For the mountains shall depart and the hills be removed, but My kindness shall not depart from you, nor shall My *covenant of peace* be removed,' says the LORD, who has mercy on you" (Isa. 54:10).

*   *   *

In the New Testament: Zechariah, the father of John the Baptist sang, "Blessed is the Lord God of Israel, For He has visited and redeemed His people . . . . And to remember His holy *covenant* the oath which He swore to our father Abraham . . ." (Luke 1:68-73). Jesus of Nazareth spoke, "Do not think that I came to destroy the Law or the Prophets [old covenant]. I did not come to destroy but to fulfill" (Matt. 5:17). "For this is My blood of the new *covenant*, which is shed for many for the remission of sins" (Matt. 26:28). Paul of Tarsus wrote, ". . . our sufficiency is from God, who also made us sufficient as ministers of the new *covenant* . . ." (2 Cor. 3:5-6). After the writer of Hebrews says that Christ is the same yesterday, today, and forever, he reminds us of the God of peace, "who brought up our Lord Jesus from the dead, that great Shepherd of the sheep, through the blood of the everlasting *covenant* . . ." (Heb. 13:8, 20). And John on Patmos heard the seventh trumpet sound. "And there were loud voices in heaven, saying, 'The kingdoms of this world have become the kingdoms of our Lord and of His Christ, and He shall reign forever and ever!' " John saw "the twenty-four elders who sat before God on their thrones," and they "fell on their faces and worshiped God, saying, 'We give You thanks, O Lord God

Almighty, the One who is and who was and who is to come' . . . , Then the temple of God was opened in heaven, and the ark of His *covenant* was seen in His temple . . ." (Rev. 11:15-19).

Thus God unveils what always has been in His heart: *The covenant of His peace*, which on the one hand redeems, on the other hand condemns.

Flock and Shepherd

Under the Old Covenant, David sang, "The LORD is my *shepherd*, I shall not want" (Ps. 23:1); Asaph prayed, "You led Your people like a *flock*" (Ps. 77:20); Isaiah prophesied, "He will feed His flock like a *shepherd*; He will gather the *lambs* with His arm, and carry them in His bosom, and gently lead those who are with *young*" (Isa. 40:11); and Ezekiel spoke, " '*I* will feed My *flock*, and *I* will make *them* lie down,' says the Lord GOD. 'I will seek what was lost and bring back what was driven away, bind up the broken and strengthen what was sick . . .' " (Ezek. 34:15-16).

Under the New Covenant: The Lord Jesus declared (isn't it as if we hear the voice of Ezekiel again?), "I am the good *shepherd*. The good *shepherd* gives His life for the *sheep* . . . . And other *sheep* I have which are not of this fold; them also I must bring, and they will hear My voice; and there will be one *flock* and one *shepherd*" (John 10:11, 16; see Ezek. 34:23-24). Paul said, "Therefore take heed to . . . all the *flock* . . . to *shepherd* the church of God . . ." (Acts 20:28). Peter exhorted, "Shepherd the *flock* of God which is among you, serving as overseers, not by compulsion but willingly, not for dishonest gain but eagerly; nor as being lords over those entrusted to you, but being examples to the *flock*; and when the Chief Shepherd appears, you will receive the crown of glory that does not fade away" (1 Pet. 5:2-4). The author to the Hebrews, as we saw above, wrote about the great *Shepherd* of the *sheep*, whom God brought back from the dead by the blood of the everlasting covenant (Heb. 13:20).

Bride

In the New Testament: "Then I, John, saw the holy city, New Jerusalem, coming down out of heaven from God, prepared as a *bride* adorned for her husband" (Rev. 21:2). "And the Spirit and the *bride* say, 'Come' " (Rev. 22:17). And the answer is, "Surely I am coming quickly" (Rev. 22:20). I am coming quickly to completely fulfill the law and the prophets, for the law and the prophets also spoke of the *bride* and the wife. Isaiah: "For your Maker is your *husband . . .*" (Isa. 54:5). Ezekiel: " 'I swore an oath to you and entered into a covenant with you, and you became Mine [i.e., My *bride*],' says the Lord GOD" (Ezek. 16:8). Hosea: "I will *betroth* you to Me forever; Yes, I will *betroth* you to Me in righteousness and justice, in lovingkindness and mercy, I will *betroth* you to Me in faithfulness . . ." (Hos. 2:19).

The language of the Old and New Testaments is one language. It is one utterance of God, who "saved us . . . through the washing of regeneration and renewing of the Holy Spirit . . . that having been justified by His grace we should become heirs according to the hope of eternal life" (Titus 3:5-7).

Heritage, inheritance, heirs — again, what comforting words, for all who belong to Christ are Abraham's seed, "heirs according to the promise" (Gal. 3:29).

What promise? The promise found in the gospel proclaimed to Abraham, "In you all the nations shall be blessed" (Gal. 3:8). Simeon saw this promise with his own eyes. When the prescribed sacrifices for newborns were brought for the child Jesus at the temple, and thereby Jesus fulfilled the law and the prophets in that way also, then Simeon could say in praise to God,

For my eyes have seen Your salvation
Which You have prepared before the face of all peoples,
A light to bring revelation to the Gentiles,
And the glory of Your people Israel (Luke 2:30-32).

Chapter Ten

THE FLOOD
AND THE RED SEA

"And [you] shall call His name JESUS" — such were the words the angel Gabriel spoke to Mary (Luke 1:31). Jesus means *Yahweh is salvation. Yahweh saves.* Gabriel (or was it another angel?) spoke the same words to Joseph, adding this explanation, "for He will save His people from their sins" (Matt. 1:21; see Matt. 28:19). He saves *His people!*

God with Us

"Now all this took place to fulfill what was spoken by the Lord through the prophet: 'Behold, the virgin shall be with child, and shall bear a Son, and they shall call His name Immanuel,' which translated means, 'God with us' " (Matt. 1:22-23; see Matt. 28:30, NASB).

God is with us again. This means we are redeemed from Satan's power and taken into fellowship with the Father (1 John 1:3). We are transported from the kingdom of darkness into the kingdom of God's beloved Son (Col. 1:13). We have passed from death into life (John 5:24). And this happens through Him who received the name Jesus from God Himself, who thus is the only "Jesus," the only Savior, the Savior of our sins (Acts 4:12). He is the one who depicts and guarantees His entire work of salvation in the sign of baptism, which is that washing of regeneration and renewal by the Holy Spirit, through which God saves us according to His mercy (Titus 3:5).

The *Flood* was an awe-inspiring event. The journey though the *Red Sea* was also awe-inspiring. But greater than both of these events is the miracle of baptism instituted by Christ.

The Flood and Baptism

The first letter of the apostle Peter was written for believers scattered over the vast region which is known today as Turkey. He called these believers chosen. They are chosen to be sprinkled with the blood of Jesus Christ (1 Pet. 1:1-2). But as chosen ones they did not have it easy. They suffered trials, slander, and threats (1 Pet. 1:6; 2:12; 3:14). Peter encourages them with words from Psalm 34:

> *For the eyes of the LORD are on the righteous,*
> *And His ears are open to their prayers;*
> *But the face of the LORD is against those who do evil*
> (1 Pet. 3:12; Ps. 34:16-17).

Thus, in a spirit of meekness and fear, with a good conscience, these believers always needed to be ready to give a defense (1 Pet. 3:15). To give a defense of what? To give a defense of the hope that is in them.

They could look to Christ with this hope, "For Christ also suffered once for sins, the just for the unjust, that He might bring us to God, being put to death in the flesh but made alive by the Spirit" (1 Pet. 3:18). Such was God's will — and Christ obeyed God's will (1 Pet. 3:17).

And what was the fruit of His obedience? God glorified Him! For being made alive by the Spirit, Christ went forth to heaven. And concerning this heavenly journey a message is proclaimed to the spirits in prison. What spirits? In what prison? Those spirits who in the days of Noah were disobedient and now find themselves in hell (1 Pet. 3:19-20).

But why specifically to them? The reason is that they are such telling examples of disobedience, of evil-doing. For they certainly had heard the preaching of Noah and witnessed the building of the ark. But they did not repent. They wished to remain completely ignorant about doing good. They were disobedient and godless (2 Pet. 2:5). Consequently they were destroyed. God sent the Flood. Only eight souls were saved — Noah and his family. Only eight!

How were these eight saved? They were "saved through water," wrote Peter (1 Pet. 3:20). The water that meant death for thousands — the water of death — became Noah's salvation.

How did the thousands die? Did they drown? No, the godless world of Noah's day was busy sinking into eternal death — that is what destroyed them. As for the Flood waters, they carried Noah and his family out of that godless world into a purified world, a world in which fellowship with the living God would again be at the forefront.

*   *   *

What a violent event! This saving *water of death*, Peter wrote, is but a picture of another water, namely, the *water of baptism* which possesses much more saving power. For the Flood is a prefiguration of baptism. That is to say, the saving water of the Flood was a prophecy of the saving water of baptism. In both we recognize the redemptive work of God (1 Pet. 3:21).

But that redemptive work speaks most strongly in baptism; it speaks most strongly in the water of baptism, which has actually transported us from death to life. Thus Christian baptism is greater than the Flood. After all, it is nothing less than a cry or prayer for a good conscience (1 Pet. 3:21).

But is a prayer, a cry, something so great? Yes, absolutely, for it is the cry of a sinner made alive unto God. It is his cry, from now on, to take part no longer in the death that reigns in the world but to serve God with a good conscience in living fellowship with him.

*   *   *

Therefore, although the chosen ones in Asia shall have to suffer, nonetheless, they are blessed (1 Pet. 3:14). They are blessed because God, according to His great mercy, has given them a new birth — through the washing of regeneration! — into a living hope, into an inheritance that is incorruptible, undefiled, and unfading, reserved in heaven for them (1 Pet. 1:3-4). Their baptism is the sign and guarantee of that inheritance. It speaks more strongly than the Flood about God's work of salvation.

The Red Sea and Baptism

First Corinthians is a letter the apostle Paul wrote to believers living in the ancient city of Corinth. These believers were at one time pagans. But now they were among those transported from death to life and incorporated into the church of the living God (1 Cor. 1:2). This happened through baptism (Acts 18:8).

They were not, however, the only people to be baptized, nor were they the first. As the apostle explained, "Moreover, brethren, I do not want you to be unaware that all our fathers were under the cloud, all passed through the sea, all were *baptized* into Moses in the cloud and in the sea" (1 Cor. 10:1-2).

Our forefathers were also baptized. When? They were baptized when they passed through the sea.

Isn't that odd? How can the apostle draw such an immediate connection between the journey through the Red Sea on the one hand, and baptism on the other? Very simply: Because he sees so clearly the powerful significance of Christian baptism. After all, baptism means nothing less than the transition from death to life. Israel experienced this transition when she passed through the sea.

We know the story: After God afflicted Egypt with ten terrible plagues, He led Israel out of the house of bondage and . . . He led them to the sea! That's when Pharaoh went into action! ". . . [H]e took six hundred choice chariots, and all the chariots of Egypt with captains over every one of them" (Ex. 14:7). He pursued Israel with these chariots and overtook them. "So they were very afraid, and the children of Israel cried out to the LORD" (Ex. 14:10) — and no wonder! The sea was in front of them — that is, death before their eyes — with the Egyptian army behind them — that is, death at their backs. Who would have given them a chance? So they cried out to the LORD and said to Moses, "Is it because there were no graves in Egypt that you have taken us away to die in the wilderness?" (Ex. 14:11, NASB).

Then it happened — the miracle! "And the Angel of God, who went before the camp of Israel, moved and went behind them; and the pillar of cloud went from before them and stood behind them.

So it came between the camp of the Egyptians and the camp of Israel" (Ex. 14:19-20). "Then Moses stretched out his hand over the sea; and the LORD caused the sea to go back by a strong east wind all that night, and made the sea into dry land, and the waters were divided. So the children of Israel went into the midst of the sea on the dry ground, and the waters were a wall to them on their right hand and on their left" (Ex. 14:21-22). "So the LORD saved Israel that day out of the hand of the Egyptians . . ." (Ex. 14:30).

*   *   *

This is the event to which Paul refers in 1 Corinthians 10. In this journey through the sea, "all our fathers were under the cloud, all passed through the sea, all were *baptized* into Moses in the cloud and in the sea" (1 Cor. 10:1-2). They were baptized into Moses (or unto Moses);[14] which is to say, by faith Israel completely entrusted herself to the leadership of Moses, the mediator of the old covenant. Israel became, so to speak, one with Moses through baptism in the cloud and the sea (Heb. 11:29; Gal. 3:19).

Moreover, in this baptism Israel crossed the boundary — the boundary between life and death — just as the Corinthians, in their baptism, crossed from the kingdom of darkness into the kingdom of God's beloved Son (Col. 1:13). In Christian baptism, God's life-saving power does not become less effectual than in that earlier baptism under the cloud and in the sea. For in the Red Sea, as with the Flood centuries before, baptism was already portrayed. It is the washing of regeneration and renewal by the Holy Spirit. It is life from the dead by God's mighty power. Just as Israel became legally free from the house of bondage in her baptism, so the church of Corinth became legally free from the bondage of sin (Ex. 20:2; Rom. 6:7).

Consequently, those who at one time were not God's people have now become, through the way of baptism, the people of God (Rom. 9:26), sanctified in Christ Jesus — for He is their Red Sea (*Belgic Confession,* art. 34) — and "called to be saints" (1 Cor. 1:2).

---

[14] See comments on page 80, note 13.

Chapter Eleven

THE PROMISE AND THE SIGN

Baptism is the washing away of sins (Acts 22:16). It is the washing of regeneration and renewal by the Holy Spirit (Titus 3:5). It is the door through which we enter the church of the living God (Matt. 28:19). Baptism is greater than the Flood and the Red Sea (1 Pet. 3:21). Such is the teaching of Scripture. And such is what we may cling to with believing hearts, for ourselves and for our children (1 Cor. 10:1-2).

Questions

Even for our children? Can these wondrous things be said even about their baptism? Some believers have difficulty with this. "Doesn't a person first have to have faith before he may be baptized?" they ask. "Didn't the Lord Jesus Himself say, 'He who believes and is baptized will be saved . . .' " (Mark 16:16)? Faith first, then baptism. Isn't that clear? Isn't that what the Lord Jesus said in the Great Commission? — ". . . make disciples of all the nations, baptizing them . . ." (Matt. 28:19). Becoming a disciple is first, then baptism. Doesn't this order hold true for the Great Commission?

Consider the biblical account regarding the Ethiopian eunuch. Philip preached the gospel of Jesus to him; and the eunuch said, "See, here is water. What hinders me from being baptized?" What reply did Philip give? He said, "If you believe with all your heart, you may" (Acts 8:36-38).

Doesn't this make the relationship between faith and baptism clear?

There is also the story of Cornelius. He came to conversion through Peter's preaching — he and the others who heard the Word. Then Peter said, "Can anyone prevent these people from being baptized with water?" And for what reason may no one prevent their baptism? — because they "have received the Holy Spirit just as we have" (Acts 10:47).

The Holy Spirit had worked faith in their hearts. Therefore Peter was not going to prevent them from being baptized and, in so doing, "withstand God" (Acts 11:17).

Still further, there is the conversion of Lydia. She was the first convert baptized on European soil. When did this happen? Only after the Holy Spirit opened her heart. Faith is first and baptism follows. This holds true with Lydia, too (Acts 16:14).

Such is also the case with the Philippian jailer. He believed and immediately, without delay, he and all his household were baptized (Acts 16:33). Isn't this how it always is: Faith comes first, with baptism following afterward?

How then can the church practice infant baptism? How can it baptize babies who are unable to believe? And then comes what some see as the decisive question: Where can you find a single verse in the Bible that says the children of believing parents ought to be baptized?

The Whole Bible

We ought not dismiss such questions (which very often are objections) as if they don't affect us, for they do affect us. Much less should we try to push them out of our minds. Such efforts leave us feeling insecure and we begin to doubt the legitimacy of our baptism. Moreover, we lose the assurance God gives us in our baptism even as young children.

So what should we do? There is only one way — by listening patiently and attentively to the teaching of the Bible, the whole Bible (Luke 24:27). This has been our goal in Chapters One through Six. We have asked for the reader's attention and patience. Now may patience receive its reward as we again turn to Scripture, for:

> *The judgments [ordinances] of the Lᴏʀᴅ*
> *Are true and righteous altogether.*
> *Moreover by them Your servant is warned,*
> *And in keeping them there is great reward* (Ps. 19:9, 11).

Only along this path do we find the biblical boldness to trust that God won't take back in the new covenant what He had given so abundantly for two thousand years in the old covenant. For what happened to Abraham? Along what path did he receive the seal of circumcision? Along the path of faith! This faith was reckoned to him as righteousness (Gen. 15:6). Subsequently(!), he received circumcision as a seal of that righteousness (Rom. 4:10-11). This is how it went with Abraham: Faith was first — just as it would be later on with the Ethiopian eunuch, and with Lydia, Cornelius, and the three thousand who were baptized on Pentecost. Only after he believed did Abraham receive circumcision as a sign, with its rich content (see Chapters Three and Four).

Again, this is just as it would be with Lydia, Cornelius, and the Philippian jailor. This is what the Lᴏʀᴅ also ordained for the old covenant. As we read: "And when a stranger dwells with you and wants to keep the Passover to the Lᴏʀᴅ, let all his males be circumcised, and then let him come near and keep it; and he shall be as a native of the land . . ." (Ex. 12:48).

Thus we see that the rule of "faith first" applied also to the stranger or alien. The alien's faith was expressed in his desire to keep the Passover to the Lᴏʀᴅ. Circumcision immediately followed and, with it, incorporation into the church of the living God. After he was circumcised, he was henceforth considered as one born in that country (also see Ps. 87:4).

This rule is no different than the one which applies under the new covenant, "If you believe with all your heart, you may [be baptized]" (Acts 8:37). This applied to the eunuch, to Cornelius, and to Lydia.

No one, in the desperate attempt to cling to the legitimacy of infant baptism, may push this divine order of "faith first" from his or her mind. Even today this rule applies to the "alien": faith first, then the sign. This divine order holds true for the old covenant and the new covenant. In the church of Jesus Christ today it is no different. Whenever an unbaptized person through missions or evangelism comes to be baptized, then the path of the alien and the eunuch is still being followed, that is, the path of "If you believe with all your heart . . . ."

God's Thoughts and Ours

It is inappropriate, however, to want to put the Lord on the short chain of our thinking; that is, to want to place our puny human thinking above His grace, above His longsuffering, above His lovingkindness and faithfulness which He keeps unto the thousandth generation (Ex. 34:6-7). After all, when the LORD placed His seal on Abraham's faith, divine mercy did not then come to an end! Even then God showed that His thoughts are not our thoughts and His ways are not our ways (of thinking). As the heavens are higher than the earth, so God's ways, already then, were higher than our ways and His thoughts than our thoughts (Isa. 55: 8-9). Then — even then — God remembered His own creation ordinances. In them He had given seed, family, generations, and nations their place. How could that divine order ever be put out of His mind (see pages 33-37)? Indeed, at the very moment God assured Abraham of His salvation with a sign, He also opened His arms to Abraham's household, to Abraham's descendants, to Abraham's people.

When God commanded Abraham to circumcise his thirteen year old son, Ishmael, and a year later to circumcise his infant son of eight days, Isaac, then God revealed that His mercy can never fit into our mental framework. We might reason that since a baby is incapable of faith, therefore(!) the child has no right to God's sign, no right even to God's promise. But the LORD revealed that He establishes His own ordinances to serve His work of salvation. God Himself had created humans in such a way that they have an ongoing history, that is, an infant grows and is nurtured unto maturity. And therefore God provides a child with parents who must instruct and lead him. And God uses this entire process of learning and development, from infancy to adulthood, in order — in that way — to form a people for Himself. After all, children belong to a people.

We have mentioned it earlier and will repeat it here: The LORD does not come upon any accidents in His work of salvation, accidents that He must then deal with the best way He can. Children, who need to mature and learn who the Lord is, are no "accident," for God Himself calls things which are not — even children — as though they were (Rom. 4:17). This holds true from the creation onward, both under the old covenant and the new covenant. Along the way of divine salvation, God omnipotently proves His mercy to thousands who love Him and keep His commandments (Ex. 20:6). He decrees marriage and sexual relations, childbirth and the full quiver, growth and development. These things do not stand outside but inside the bright and warm sphere of His covenant of grace. In this covenant God gives His peace and proclaims His peace — even peace on those who are near to Him in this covenant, near to Him who assures them with a promise and a sign that He is their God (Eph. 2:13, 17; Isa. 57:19; Gen. 17:7).

What more can anyone want? What more can one receive than to be able to grow up near to God in this way, in this path? The book of Proverbs says many good things about this. Neither a waterfall of words nor rivers of ink can blot out the fact that God has proved Himself to be the covenant God of little children.

*   *   *

And if we, now that the new dispensation has come, should want to fence the greatness of God's mercy within the narrow borders of what seems good and possible to us, then we are on the wrong road. We are on a road of foolishness, for then we will understand neither the Scriptures nor the power of God (Mark 12:24, 27). On that road we will seriously err. We will dishonor God (yes, dishonor), for on that road we will conceive of God — the God who is great in mercy and remembers His covenant through the centuries, the God who is mindful of the word that He commanded for a thousand generations (Ps. 105:8) — we will conceive of that God as too small.

The Anchor of Our Faith?

What are the consequences of such thinking? If we think too little of God, we inevitably think too much of ourselves. We think too much of the boundaries that we fancy we need to draw. We also think too much of our faith. We think we must first give baptism its validity. We think our baptism must first be given its legal force. And this happens not only at the moment we let ourselves be baptized as adults, not only at that day or hour, but also years later, a whole lifetime later. Our faith must continually become the legal basis of the promise that God gives. It must even become the legal basis for the seal of His promise. Our faith must become the legal basis for the guarantee of the washing away of sins, the guarantee of the Holy Spirit's work of regeneration and renewal. Our faith must become the legal basis for membership in the church of the living God. In other words, our faith must become the anchor for our souls, replacing the hope that is sure and anchored firmly in God's unwavering faithfulness, as we are taught in Scripture (Heb. 6:17-19).

If our faith becomes the anchor for our souls, then in prosperity and adversity, in life's bloom and life's decline, yes, even on our deathbeds, we have to find rest, not in the unchanging character of God's gracious covenant, but in the shifting sands of what is happening or once has happened in our own hearts — both faith and unbelief, certainty and doubt, hope and despair, joy and uncertainty.

We come to such a view if we lack humility. After all, humility wants to know nothing except what God has revealed to us in all of Scripture, what He has revealed concerning His lovingkindness, a lovingkindness that He continues to show to thousands (Ex. 34:6-7).

Is God a God of adults alone? Is He not a God of infants? Yes, He is also a God of children and infants, from whose mouths He has perfected praise (Matt. 21:16; Ps. 8:2). God declared this very thing to Abraham and his descendants under the old covenant (Gen. 17:7). The hands of the Lord Jesus, extended in blessing, confirmed it in the transition period from the old covenant to the new (Luke 18:15-17). And the apostle's words proclaimed it in the new covenant when he said that the children in the congregation are holy (1 Cor. 7:14). This is why earlier in the same letter he had addressed them as "sanctified in Christ Jesus" and as "called to be saints" (1 Cor. 1:2). They are blessed children.

Faith Unnecessary?

But if such great blessings are sealed and guaranteed also in the baptism of small children, doesn't baptism then render faith unnecessary? And if it doesn't render faith unnecessary, what is the place and meaning of faith in a living relationship with God?

We can best begin to answer these questions by posing a couple of counter-questions. Does the seal on a letter make the reception of that letter unnecessary, so that the recipient need not pay attention to the content of the letter? Obviously not! In fact, the seal confirms the letter. The seal is precisely what requires the recipient to take even more careful account of what that letter says.

Does the signature of the President or Prime Minister on a piece of legislation make obedience to that law unnecessary? Of course it doesn't. On the contrary, the signature of the head of state, signing a bill into law, places a heavier obligation upon us to obey. In a just state, a law that is signed by its highest official may not be slighted.

Well then, would the sign of God's promise make the requirement of that promise unnecessary — that is, that every *promise*, according to its nature, requires *faith*? Understand, the promise and sign do not produce careless and godless people who go about blithely thinking all is well with them because, after all, they were baptized as children. Absolutely not! Whoever thinks like that has not understood anything about infant baptism.

How could the very people who receive God's promise live without faith in that promise, especially since God has laid that promise so heavily upon their hearts through their baptism? In fact, they live only because they have not rent asunder what God has joined together (Matt. 19:6). They neither separate the sign from the promise nor the promise from faith. Indeed, we must hold firmly to all of the words of the author and finisher of our faith (Heb. 12:2), which include, "He who believes and is baptized will be saved" (Mark 16:16a), and the words that immediately follow, "but he who does not believe will be condemned" (Mark 16:16b).

The unbeliever will be condemned even if he has been baptized in rivers of water, whether as a child or as an adult. But we may hold no less firmly to another word of the Lord Jesus, and to the deed that He adds to it. By this word, as with all His words and deeds, He fulfills the law and the prophets, namely, "Let the little children come to Me, and do not forbid them; for of such is the kingdom of God . . . . And He took them up in His arms, put His hands on them, and blessed them" (Mark 10:14, 16). How then could anyone withhold the water of baptism from such ones to whom Christ promised the kingdom of God (Acts 10:47)?

We must cling tightly to the one and we must cling tightly to the other. After all, we know, not on the basis of our logical deductions but only on the basis of God's Word, that baptizing the church's children does not make faith unnecessary; rather, the opposite, baptism makes faith more necessary. We must allow ourselves to be instructed in these matters by that Word!

By Faith

What is then the role and meaning of faith? When the Bible says that we are justified by faith, that we are saved by faith, and that we live by faith, what does that mean (Rom. 3:28; 1:16-17)? Scripture gives us the answer from what it teaches us about Abraham, the father of all believers (Rom. 4:16).

Since Sarah was barren, Abraham's marriage remained childless (Gen. 11:30). The LORD, however, promised Abraham that He would make him a great nation (Gen. 12:2). The LORD gave him the sign of the stars, saying, "So shall your descendants be" (Gen. 15:5).

Abraham, as well as Sarah, deemed these words of promise from the LORD as *trustworthy*. He accepted God's Word and held it for *truth* (Heb. 11:11). That is faith. That is the meaning of faith — it *rests* in the Word of the Lord. Abraham lived for years after this manner: As one seeing what could not yet be seen. He realized that his own body was dead, for he was about one hundred years old. He certainly considered Sarah's womb to be dead. She was almost ninety years old.

Yet, despite this, Abraham gave glory to God (Rom. 4:19-20). He glorified God by building the house of his life on the foundation of God's unshakable Word. He rested on this very last footing — that it was *impossible that God should lie* (Heb. 6:18). Indeed, faith is certainty of things hoped for; the evidence of things not seen (Heb. 11:1). Just as the field absorbs the rain, and the sun shines upon it and blesses it, so faith lets itself be addressed and blessed by God, in whom it firmly trusts.

The LORD taught Israel to live by faith when, while living decades in the wilderness, they were not allowed to stock up a supply of manna but each day anew had to trust God that He would again provide enough the following day (Ex. 16). Abel, Enoch, Noah, and all the heros of faith mentioned in the eleventh chapter of Hebrews, each gave glory to God and deemed God's promises to be unshakable. And God was willing to reckon that trusting in Him, that holding for true, that resting in Him, and that building on His Word, as righteousness.

Why? Was it because Abraham had earned it in view of the difficult path he walked? No, that wasn't the reason. There is no talk of merit, for even the faith of Abraham was God's own work and God's own gift (Eph. 2:8). So why, then? It was because God wanted, in this way, to open up the *depth of the riches of His mercy* to Abraham and His descendants (Rom. 11:33).

Therefore, as mentioned earlier, for reasons of His own and in unfathomable mercy, God reckoned Abraham's faith as righteousness. God reckons our faith as righteousness, too (Rom. 4:24). Salvation is by grace alone. Abraham could not have invented that. Nobody has merited it. Nobody could have obliged God to do it. But what no eye had seen, what no ear had heard, and what no human heart had conceived, God prepared for those who love Him

— that is, righteousness by faith (1 Cor. 2:9). Such faith lives by God's promise and from God's promise. Just as we can live only in an environment that has oxygen for our lungs, so faith can live only in the climate of promise. In that climate faith does not think too much of itself.

Thus, when God puts forward a sign and a seal because of the weakness of our faith, then even in the sign and seal faith directs itself to the activity of God. Isn't it then presumptuous, on the one hand, to consider the sign insignificant and say, "I have the promise, that is enough. What can a sign do for me?" On the contrary, by having the promise faith itself reaches out for the sign, "See, here is water. What hinders me from being baptized?" (Acts 8:36). Yet, on the other hand, faith also does not arbitrarily separate the sign from the promise in order then to run wild with the sign and say something like this: "Once baptized, always saved — what can happen to me?"

What God Has Joined Together . . .

Both of these notions cast disparagement upon the sign. The first is held by people who think that they are saved by their own efforts. Consequently, they have no need for the church of the living God with its official functions — the administration of baptism, for example.

They must know that in doing this they are not receiving the Word of God in faith. After all, in the letters of the apostles the Lord does not address individuals but churches — see, for example, 1 Cor. 1:2; 2 Cor. 1:1; Gal. 1:2; also see Christ's letters to the seven churches in Revelation 2 and 3. In the letter to the Hebrews, the Lord also admonishes His people, in so many words, not to neglect gathering together among themselves — which is not an incidental exhortation to go faithfully to church. Look how it fits with the chapter.

In Hebrews 10, meeting together as believers has to do with the full assurance of faith; it has to do with our hearts which are sprinkled clean from an evil conscience; it has to do with our bodies which are washed with pure water (Heb. 10:22). Baptism is in view here! Proceeding from all of that, the author then states that we must hold fast to this confession, and we must spur each other on in this confession. And that's why we must not neglect our own gathering together, with its official administrations, since there, in such gatherings, all of that is proclaimed to us and sealed in the sacraments of baptism and the Lord's Supper (Heb. 10:19-25).

*   *   *

Perhaps we think: No such danger threatens us, for we go to church every Sunday. We do not think lightly of the church's official administrations, including baptism.

Is that really true? Do we really think much of the sign God gives to our children when we so easily postpone the administration of it until this or that Sunday when all our aunts and uncles can attend the baptism service? Moreover, how much do we think of the sign when it has our attention only on that particular Sunday but then is seldom if ever considered — or applied further down the road — in our children's education, in choice of schools, in one's own life?

We must not think to exalt our courtesy (to relatives) above the *exhortation* to strive for holiness, "having our hearts sprinkled from an evil conscience and our bodies washed [— in baptism —] with pure water" (Heb. 10:22).

So much for the first notion.

The second notion consists of *swearing* by the sign apart from the word of promise — Israel did not escape that evil. She talked up circumcision to the heights of heaven, but in a unspiritual manner. Thus, is not what Paul wrote aimed at them? "If you break the law [— the law which is so closely tied to the promise —], your circumcision has become uncircumcision" (Rom. 2:25). And a little further, "nor is circumcision that which is outward in the flesh; but . . . circumcision is that of the heart, in the Spirit, not in the letter . . ." (Rom. 2:28-29). Moreover, it can even happen that the apostle speaks of "the so-called 'Circumcision,' which is performed in the flesh by human hands" (Eph. 2:11, NASB).

In these passages does Paul think lightly of the sign that God Himself had instituted? Does he oppose the Old Testament?

Absolutely not! Instead he actually holds fast to the true meaning of circumcision, the true meaning that is grasped by faith alone, that does not separate what God has joined together. Thus he follows exactly and completely in line with the old covenant — with Deuteronomy: "Therefore circumcise the foreskin of your heart, and be stiff-necked no longer" (Deut. 10:16); with Jeremiah: "Circumcise yourselves to the LORD, and take away the foreskins of your hearts . . ." (Jer. 4:4).

And if in the new dispensation the same sin should appear among us as appeared among Israel, if we should also run wild with the sign, separating it from the promise, and if we should view our baptism or the baptism of our children at all like a passport that cannot expire, then these words would have to be aimed at us: ". . . neither is baptism that which is outward in the flesh. But . . . true baptism is that of the heart which is sprinkled clean from an evil conscience, by the Spirit, not by the letter" (see Rom. 2:28-29; Heb. 10:22).

Promise and Faith

On the one hand, faith must daily allow itself to be certain of the trustworthiness of the promise through the sign. On the other, the sign must daily let itself be explained through the promise. Faith does not wrench the one loose from the other — neither the sign from the promise, nor the promise from the sign.

To be sure, in the Bible baptism is called the washing away of sins. But how are we to understand that? We must understand it as the guarantee attached to the *promise* — the promise that God forgives us our sins through Christ's blood and Spirit. This *promise* requires *faith*. Such is the case with every word of promise.

In Scripture baptism is called the washing of regeneration and renewal by the Holy Spirit. This is clear. But how are we to understand that? Again, we must understand it as a seal attached to the *promise* — the promise that God regenerates and renews by His

Spirit. And that *promise* requires *faith*. Such is the case with every word of promise.

Baptism is the door through which we enter the church of the living God. This is certain. But we have to understand that biblically. Again, baptism functions as a guarantee attached to the *promise* — the promise that God incorporates us into the church and will keep us there our whole life long. And that *promise* requires *faith*, as is the case with every promise.

Baptism is more than the Flood and the journey through the Red Sea. But how? As something automatic? As something natural? No! Rather, again, only as a seal attached to the *promise* — the promise that God delivers us from the godless world and transports us into the kingdom of His Son, the promise that He delivers us from the house of bondage, the house of sin, and frees us for His service. And this *promise* requires *faith*, an unwavering faith, a faith that stands firm in all circumstances.

Baptism does not foster false peace of mind or proud self-sufficiency. Pay attention and read carefully. In what context does the apostle call baptism the washing of regeneration and renewal by the Holy Spirit? Paul does that in the context of urging Titus to admonish the churches on the island of Crete to be diligent in good works and to excel in them. Good works are works of faith. Baptism does not switch off faith (Titus 3:1-8).

In what context does Peter call baptism the antitype of the Flood? He does so in the context of warning the believers to do their best in what is good so that they may be prepared to give a defense to all who ask for the reason of the *hope* that is in them, so that they may walk well in Christ, and so that they may no longer live according to human desires but live according to the will of God. How would a person be able to do all of that apart from faith (1 Pet. 3-5)?

And in what context did Paul speak about the baptism of Israel in the cloud and in the sea? He did that in the framework of admonitions and warnings. He admonished believers to run the race of faith in such a way that they may win the prize. That admonition to run is quite different from a walk of proud self-assurance. He warned them not to lust after evil, as Israel did, not to be idolaters as some in Israel were, not to commit sexual immorality as some of them did — and twenty-three thousand fell in a single day — and not to tempt the Lord, as some of them did, and were destroyed by serpents.

These things happened to them, wrote the apostle, as an example for us; and they were written down to warn us. Therefore, if you think you are standing (as in false peace of mind on account of your baptism), watch out that you do not fall (see 1 Cor. 9:24-10:13)!

This is what the Bible teaches us about the meaning and force of baptism and promise; it shows us the way of faith.

Wholesome Instruction

That instruction is the cure for all unhealthy views, from the one side or the other. It is the cure for the notion — whether expressed in so many words or not — that our faith should make us worthy of baptism, that our faith should provide the legal basis and force for our baptism.

Whoever thinks that way is on a deadly path — again, whether that idea is expressed or is only present in the back of one's mind. After all, we must bring into proper view what that would mean: To maintain that children have no right to the sign that seals the promise means children have no right to the promise itself. Is baptism invalid before we believe? If so, then the promise is also without force before we believe. And if that is how we construe the relationship between God and ourselves, then we run a great and deadly danger. Indeed, we come terribly close — not to say it too strongly — to an ancient heresy, namely, that our redemption is not the work of God alone but that we offer and contribute our faith to the work of redemption, that our faith supplies the last ingredient, thus making us worthy of the promise and its guarantee.

But righteousness through faith, salvation through faith, building the house of our life-of-faith on the rock of God's Word, doesn't mean that God, from His side, has done perhaps 99.9 percent, and that we, from our side, still have to supply the last tenth, hundredth, or thousandth percent. It doesn't mean that we, thanks to our final minimal contribution, finally acquire the right to the promise and its accompanying sign. No, God Himself has laid the legal basis for the promise — God alone, God completely, God who works in us both the willing and the working (Phil. 2:13).

Considering God Faithful

Now if someone still asks, seriously asks, "What then is the place and function of faith in the relationship between God and humans," then the answer, once more, is nothing other than that we consider God faithful (Heb. 11:11), nothing other than that we hold for truth what God has said (John 3:33), nothing other than that we accept what He has promised (Heb. 11:13), nothing other than that we drink in the blessing of His grace, nothing other than that we are illuminated by the light of His countenance (Num. 6:25).

Faith is the path along which God's blessing comes to us — an essential path — but a path that is God's gift. Faith is the hand that accepts what God gives — an indispensable hand — but a hand that God Himself has created. No one has such faith of himself. No one earns faith by merit. It is, from beginning to end, from God and through God and to God (Rom. 11:36).

Where then is the worthiness of faith? It is excluded. "He who glories, let him glory in the LORD" (1 Cor. 1:31).

Chapter Twelve

WHERE DOES IT SAY THAT?

But where in the Bible does it say that baptism has replaced circumcision? That's the first question. And the second is this: Where does it say that little children should be baptized?

For many believers the answers to these types of questions are decisive, more decisive unfortunately than the *total witness* of the entire Bible. And that is true not only with respect to baptism.

There are people (Christian people!) who live together as husband and wife. In the eyes of the law, however, they are not married. If someone tells them that this is not the Lord's will, then the question is asked, "Where in the Bible does it say you have to be legally married in order to live together as husband and wife?" For them, it is a question that is already answered. They are more than ready to say, "Nowhere!" That is their claim, while in abundantly plain language the entire testimony of Scripture, from Genesis 2:24 to Revelation 21:9, tells us otherwise. But they are looking for the answer from only one or two verses, from a specific command or prohibition, while we must live by all of Scripture.

Significant Silence

In this book our attention has been directed to God's Word in order that we might find an answer to the first question mentioned above. We refer particularly to Chapters Two through Six and pages 82-86 of Chapter Eight. With the explanation provided in those pages, that question has been answered, for baptism has indeed replaced circumcision. What remains to be considered is whether children have the right to the promise and to the sign of the promise. In order to help overcome doubt and uncertainty, we still want to consider the second question. Again, it follows from the whole testimony of Scripture that there is certainly more to say about that than this book has expressed up to this point.

We begin by acknowledging that *nowhere* in the Bible do we find a verse which prescribes, in so many words, that the children of believing parents are candidates for baptism. Moreover, *nowhere* in the Bible do we find a verse that says, in so many words, that children in a specific case were baptized. We acknowledge that up front.

But we immediately add that *nowhere* in the Bible do we find a verse that says that the children of believing parents definitely ought not to be baptized or that the children of believing parents are excluded from baptism. Moreover, *nowhere* do we find that the children of believing parents, upon reaching maturity, yet needed to be baptized. In light of that last statement, could one have any justification for concluding that these children, when they were still small, were not baptized?

Perhaps one finds that these observations say very little. But then we ask, "Doesn't it actually mean a great deal that the baptism of little children is not mentioned, in so many words, in the New Testament? Or is that, perhaps, what is precisely very significant?" Our answer is that it is very significant.

Let's consider the situation a little further. For two thousand years Israel had to live according to the covenant promise: I am your God and the God of your descendants. For two thousand years the little boys in Israel were circumcised on the basis of that promise. They had received the seal of the righteousness by faith and thereby they were incorporated into the people of God (Rom. 4:11; Gen. 17:12).

In this way the LORD had His lofty thoughts indelibly etched into the conscience and thinking of His people. They knew nothing else. And now, on the great day of Pentecost, three thousand members of that people are baptized — three thousand covenant children who had heard and learned and known nothing else than this: God is not only a God of adults but also of their children.

Now what were those baptized Jews supposed to think? Were they supposed to think that God had suddenly removed His covenant law? Were they supposed to think that He had changed, that their God had changed, whom they knew as Yahweh, as I AM WHO I AM, as the One who is the first, also in the covenant, and is the same with the last (Isa. 41:4)?

Remember, the temple ministry was over. The Lord had clearly demonstrated that when He ripped the veil of the temple in two from top to bottom (Matt. 27:51). What God was saying with the outpouring of the Holy Spirit was also clear, for that event did not take place in the temple. The Spirit did not descend upon the priesthood — a priesthood that was at least fourteen-hundred years old. No, rather, the Spirit descended upon that small group of people, in some obscure room, the location of which we cannot be certain (Acts 2:1).

In both of those events the Lord was speaking clearly, namely, from now on the path of salvation will no longer run through the temple and its priestly ministry. Believers do not have to be in doubt about that.

God established the line of the covenant, which was approximately six-hundred years older than the Levitical priesthood and tabernacle (or temple) service — thus possibly six-hundred years more deeply etched into the conscience of God's people. Thus is it not more than significant that God gives no indication that henceforth this principle of the covenant and its sign would no longer be valid, the principle of "you and your descendants"? Isn't it more than significant that not a word is said about that?

Significant Speaking

But is it really so that not a word is said about it? Not a word? On the great day of Pentecost was nothing actually said about the *children* of believing parents? On the contrary, when the Jewish men asked, in the language of the covenant (!), "Men and brethren, what shall we do?" then what is Peter's answer? He said, "Repent, and let everyone of you be baptized . . . . for the promise is to you . . ." (Acts 2:37-39).

But the apostle goes further. And who come into view? The children! They are mentioned, yes, "in so many words": "For the promise is to you *and to your children* . . ." (Acts 2:39). That is the old language of the old covenant: to be a God to you and to your descendants. For that matter, the next phrase (by the way) is also the old language and the old line, as Peter goes on and says, ". . . and to all who are afar off, as many as the Lord our God will call" (Acts 2:39). That phrase, too, runs completely parallel to the Abrahamic promise which was for all the families of the earth (Gen. 12:3; Rom. 4:17; Gal. 3:8).

No, none of us may say that on the day of Pentecost, when the break-through from the old dispensation into the new became a reality, that no attention was paid to the children or that no word was directed to them. On the contrary, under the old covenant God was always the God of adults and of their children. He would also be such under the new covenant. A lot of words were not needed to get this across to the "men and brethren." By God's goodness it was, so to speak, right at their feet.

If it had been otherwise, would not God have told Israel and us? That is to say, if from Pentecost onward children actually no longer belonged to the line of the covenant, if God had actually changed — the God who gave Abraham and Israel specific commands about circumcision (Gen. 17:9-14; Ex. 12:48), and who even paid attention to the "loops" and "clasps" of the tabernacle (Ex. 26:1-6) — would He not have told Israel and us? Would God have left it to our limited insight and small minds to discern that great reversal within Himself?

Besides, hasn't God spoken? Hasn't He spoken clearly? Hasn't He included the children in His speaking? "For the promise is to you and to your children . . ." (Acts 2:39) — even as His Son, His beloved, spoke clearly and acted accordingly, "Let the little children come to Me, and do not forbid them; for of such is the kingdom of

God . . . And He took them up in His arms, put His hands on them, and blessed them" (Mark 10:14, 16).

Significant Actions

The passages that talk about the baptism of Lydia (Acts 16:15), the Philippian jailer (Acts 16:33), Crispus (Acts 18:8), and Stephanas (1 Cor. 1:16; 16:15), and their households receive their proper place when we see them in the light of the ongoing line of the covenant. Indeed, Paul's words to the jailer do not seem strange when seen in that light. Instead, within the context of the entire message of Scripture, they become very significant.

When the jailer asked what he must do to be saved, then the apostle answered, "Believe on the Lord Jesus Christ, and you will be saved, you and your household" (Acts 16:31). Notice that Paul speaks in the singular person! His words are intended for one man, the jailer. And when that one man puts his faith in the Lord Jesus, then he must be baptized at once, along with his household. Yes, for the promise is to him *and to his household.*

Compare that to what the LORD said in the old covenant about the stranger who wanted to observe the Passover (see Ex. 12:48). We do not need to repeat it here. Compare and consider whether it is not the same language and the same covenant-principle that is now being applied to the Philippian jailer and his household. The same can be said of Crispus, that he came to faith *with all his household* (Acts 18:8), just as the stranger of Exodus 12.

Probabilities?

But someone might say in reply: Yes, but who says that there were children in these four households — of Lydia, the Philippian jailer, Crispus, and Stephanas? Isn't it possible that they were all grown adults?

Yes, and what isn't possible?

But then one has to make a number of assumptions — first, that there were no children, let's say under the age of twelve, in those four households; and more, that the adults in those four households, man for man, woman for woman, servant for servant, all came to faith together at the same time.

Isn't that possible? Certainly it's possible. But it could have happened another way. In fact it did happen another way.

Consider what Paul wrote about households having a believing husband and an unbelieving wife, or vice versa. In such situations, if we really must weigh probabilities, then chances are much more likely that the children in such households were baptized (with the believing parent) than that only the adults were baptized (1 Cor. 7:10-16). Isn't this in keeping with the witness of all of Scripture?

Holy Children

We will not repeat now what we said earlier in Chapter Seven about Paul seeing children as belonging to the church of the living God (see pages 55-61). Neither will we repeat our discussion on the circumcision of Christ (see pages 82-84). But we do want to consider carefully the teaching the apostle gives us from 1 Corinthians 7: "For the unbelieving husband is sanctified by the wife, and the unbelieving wife is sanctified by the husband; otherwise your children would be unclean, but now *they are holy*" (1 Cor. 7:14).

What concerns us now are those last, italicized words. In what context do those words arise?

This chapter deals with married couples, involving one partner who has become a believer while the other partner remains an unbeliever. Questions arise in such circumstances: How must the believing party cope with such a situation? Could a believing husband yet remain with his unbelieving wife? Could a believing mother yet remain with her family — with her husband and children? Could someone clean remain with someone unclean — a believer in a circle of unbelief?

Or should the marriage and the family be ended for the Lord? Does the Lord require, for His sake, that the bonds He Himself instituted be rent asunder, the bonds between husband and wife, between parents and children? No, that is not His will. What God has first joined together, He does not rent asunder (see pages 33-37). If the unbelieving party agrees to remain in the relationship, then the believing husband or wife should accept that situation (1 Cor. 7:12-13); and if they have children together, then the believing father need not forfeit his duties to raise them, and then the believing mother can pray for her children, and even pray with her children. Thus the Lord performs His work of sanctification in that household. The unbelieving husband is made holy through the wife; the unbelieving wife is made holy through the husband.

The power of God's grace is so strong that the apostle doesn't merely say that the children from such a situation are *not unclean* but, much more, that they are *holy. Holy* — that is to say, they are set apart by the Lord and for the Lord. The Lord has laid His hand on them.

*   *   *

What do we learn from this with respect to the question of infant baptism? We learn that if children who come from such a fractured family are holy, then children whose father and mother are both believers are surely likewise holy. We learn that if parents are members of the church of the living God, then their children are members as well. If the parents are blessed, then the children are also blessed. Their children, already at birth, are not excluded from citizenship in Israel; they are not aliens to the covenant of promise, without Christ, without God, and without hope in the world (Eph. 2:11-12).

God makes no separation between parents and children. He doesn't receive parents into fellowship with Himself but exclude their children — as if their children were stray souls. He did not create their children in that way, thus neither will He treat them in that way. Children, with their parents, have been brought near by the blood of Christ (Eph. 2:13). And there is such comfort, such an anchor, according to 1 Corinthians 7:14, even for families suffering such a painful rift.

To be sure, the apostle is not dealing with baptism here. But the light — that is, the light of revelation — does shine here on the position of children in the church. And their position is no different than what it was under the old covenant, no different than what it was during the time of the Lord Jesus and His earthly ministry (Mark 10:13-16). Children do not stand outside the circle of salvation. They are not afar off but nearby. The promise comes to them and, along with it, the sign, the guarantee of the promise (Eph. 2:13, 17; Gen. 17:9-14).

Resting in Scripture

Where does it say that the children of believing parents ought to be baptized? Some people will not be at rest with the question of infant baptism until they can find a verse that expressly commands or forbids it. Whoever is like that will never find rest.

But whoever allows himself to be taught by all of Scripture — by Moses, by the prophets, by God's Son, and by the apostles — need not live in uncertainty (Luke 24:27; 16:31; Heb. 1:1). He need not be uncertain regarding the position of children in the church — not regarding their baptism, not regarding his own baptism, even if we were baptized in the first week of our lives. What God has promised remains in force, even for a lifetime.

Chapter Thirteen

A SIGN FOR WHICH TO BE THANKFUL

People give each other signs — wedding rings, for example. But *there is so little fidelity in the world*. The value of human words or signs is never greater than the faithfulness of the one who stands behind them. We know full well that often little remains of our words and signs.

A Sign of Faithfulness

When God, however, makes a promise and joins a sign to it, whether at some later point in our lives or already at birth, then that *sign*ified promise remains in effect, and the strong effect of that can accompany us through the days and years of our lives, as long as we live. God stands behind it. He stands behind His word and behind His sign —

a sign of faithfulness for all who seek salvation in Him alone,
a sign of faithfulness for us when we are weak in faith,
a sign of faithfulness when we have fallen into sin (again!),
a sign of faithfulness when we must confess once more that nothing
    good dwells in us, that is, in our flesh (Rom. 7:18),
a sign of faithfulness when we are young and worry whether God
    can forgive sinners like ourselves,
a sign of faithfulness when we, at middle age, have not always gone
    the way we know we should have gone,
a sign of faithfulness for parents who are blessed with children and
    seek to raise them, who have to bury a child, or even
    sometimes see a child straying away from the LORD,
a sign of faithfulness when our lives are blossoming,

a sign of God's faithfulness when we must continually go about
    weighed down with difficulties,
a sign for each of us in all life's circumstances,
a sign even when we draw near to death,
a trustworthy sign,
a sign for which to be thankful.

Giving Thanks

Let us give thanks with the church of Christ, with the community
of the living God:

Almighty, merciful God and Father,
we thank and praise Thee
that Thou hast forgiven
us and our children all our sins
through the blood of Thy beloved Son Jesus Christ.
Thou hast received us
through Thy Holy Spirit
as members of Thy only-begotten Son,
and so adopted us to be Thy children.
Thou hast sealed and confirmed this
to us by holy baptism.
We beseech Thee through Thy beloved Son
that Thou wilt always govern us
by Thy Holy Spirit,
that we may live a truly Christian and godly life
and grow and increase in the Lord Jesus Christ.
Grant that we may acknowledge
Thy fatherly goodness and mercy,
which Thou hast shown to us all.
May we live in all righteousness
under our only Teacher,
King, and High Priest, Jesus Christ,
and valiantly fight against and overcome

sin, the devil, and his whole dominion.
May we forever praise and magnify
Thee and Thy Son Jesus Christ,
together with the Holy Spirit,
the one only true God. Amen.[15]

That is a prayer to say "*amen*" to every day.

---

[15] See "Form for the Baptism of Adults," *Book of Praise: Anglo-Genevan Psalter*, p. 592.

SCRIPTURE INDEX